Management for Professionals

Bergamin and Braun's illustration of how integration projects can be planned and implemented successfully is the result of their own experiences of around 30 M&A transactions from different industries. Their practical approach also features in-depth interviews that are based on the findings of their research.

More information about this series at http://www.springer.com/series/10101

Stephan Bergamin • Markus Braun

Mergers and Acquisitions

Integration and Transformation
Management as the Gateway to Success

Stephan Bergamin
Männedorf, Switzerland

Markus Braun
Winterthur, Switzerland

Originally published with the title M&A: Erfolg dank Integrationsmanagement. Herausforderungen, Erfahrungsberichte, Praktikerleitfaden by Verlag Neue Zürcher Zeitung, 2015

ISSN 2192-8096 ISSN 2192-810X (electronic)
Management for Professionals
ISBN 978-3-319-60503-6 ISBN 978-3-319-60504-3 (eBook)
DOI 10.1007/978-3-319-60504-3

Library of Congress Control Number: 2017942801

© Springer International Publishing AG 2018
This work is subject to copyright. All rights are reserved by the Publisher, whether the whole or part of the material is concerned, specifically the rights of translation, reprinting, reuse of illustrations, recitation, broadcasting, reproduction on microfilms or in any other physical way, and transmission or information storage and retrieval, electronic adaptation, computer software, or by similar or dissimilar methodology now known or hereafter developed.
The use of general descriptive names, registered names, trademarks, service marks, etc. in this publication does not imply, even in the absence of a specific statement, that such names are exempt from the relevant protective laws and regulations and therefore free for general use.
The publisher, the authors and the editors are safe to assume that the advice and information in this book are believed to be true and accurate at the date of publication. Neither the publisher nor the authors or the editors give a warranty, express or implied, with respect to the material contained herein or for any errors or omissions that may have been made. The publisher remains neutral with regard to jurisdictional claims in published maps and institutional affiliations.

Printed on acid-free paper

This Springer imprint is published by Springer Nature
The registered company is Springer International Publishing AG
The registered company address is: Gewerbestrasse 11, 6330 Cham, Switzerland

Preface

Mergers and acquisitions have become the order of the day. Not a week goes by without a new M&A deal hitting the headlines in the business news: LafargeHolcim, dormakaba, Gate Group and HNA, Syngenta and ChemChina, to name just a few transactions that have made quite a splash in recent weeks and months. They clearly demonstrate that global business transformation is more than a buzzword, but actually sine qua non for many businesses to stand the test of time amidst their international competitors. Technological development and the demand for access to new purchasing and sales markets are turning the economy upside down. Traditional courses of action and patterns of behavior are losing their impact. New competitors, elevated cost structures, alternative technologies, and new markets are merely a few triggers of an urgent transformation process. Small to large businesses all have to decide whether they should keep struggling single handedly or join forces to become stronger and more efficient.

There is a need for agile business organizations that are characterized by *speed and flexibility, and their openness to change around them.*

Our experience of many years as CFOs and managers with operative responsibility combined with academic research has enabled us to identify similar patterns that in many cases are paramount to the success of a business transformation. The following presents a list of these factors:

1. Identify the *need for change* and communicate its urgency.
2. *Accountability* must be ensured and *guiding coalitions* be built from the start; in other words, an aligned management is able to drive fundamental changes in the company.
3. *Implement changes perceptively and stringently*: An organization requires change agents to implement changes. The necessity for change must be universally acknowledged for overall support.
4. *The right spirit* certainly helps to put the entire organization in motion.

Business transformations are often closely linked with *M&A transactions*. A company's global strategy is deliberately and rapidly promoted by external growth. M&A transactions thereby are more than mere triggers or the answer to business transformation; a successful M&A transaction depends on whether any

Fig. 1 Typical steps in change management. Source: Bergamin/Braun

subsequent integration management follows the guidelines of a business transformation.

What are the most important considerations? What success factors and obstacles promote or hamper a successful merger? Merging with another company on paper or purchasing it is one thing, but any future value added can only be achieved when different company cultures are combined to forge a single powerful unit.

Growing globalization in the economy has spawned a multitude of cross-border transactions: Commerzbank, Kuka Robotics, Champions League finalist Atlético Madrid, Syngenta, Gate Group, Swissport, SR Technics; what do they have in common? All these companies have passed into Chinese ownership in recent years. The management will certainly have experienced that there is one aspect beyond the gift of perceptibility, speed, and flexibility that takes center stage in successful business transactions: openness for other cultures and mentalities.

What are the deal breakers? How can an integration process be successfully kick-started and managed? What challenges are there with respect to different cultures and mentalities? As managers and CFOs, the authors have personally mentored close to 30 M&A transactions. This book is an account of their experiences and a handbook for successful integration management.

The following investigates three aspects:

1. What are the key factors for success or failure of integration management in M&A projects?
2. What courses of action have revealed to be successful with performance transformation during the integration process?
3. How do global players tackle integration management? Those in charge of the mergers of dormakaba and LafargeHolcim demonstrate in an exhilarating way how they proceeded in their merger process.

We trust that the practical advice and checklists in this book can be put to good use in your day-to-day work.

We would like to express our gratitude to and profound respect for our interview partners Riet Cadonau, Christof Hässig, Walter Oberhänsli, Hans Hess, Renato Fassbind, Philippe Hertig and Wolfgang Werlé; experts Philipp Robinson and Stefan Rösch-Rütsche and Samy Walleyo. We are thankful for their valuable contributions and the many rewarding discussions. We also thank Petra Hanselmann for the chapter on the legal aspects of a merger.

Männedorf, Switzerland　　　　　　　　　　　　　　　　　　Stephan Bergamin
Winterthur, Switzerland　　　　　　　　　　　　　　　　　　　　Markus Braun

Contents

1 Integration Management in Mergers and Acquisitions: Success Factors and Pitfalls.................................. 1
2 Integration Management as a Gateway to Performance Transformation.. 33
3 Global Merger *dormakaba*: Interview and Case Study............ 73
4 Global Merger *LafargeHolcim*: Interview and Case Study......... 87

Closing Remarks... 95

Glossary.. 97

About the Authors

Stephan Bergamin holds a Ph.D. in Economics from HSG University of St. Gallen (Switzerland), studied business administration at the University of St. Gallen, and holds an AMP from Harvard University. He is CFO of Gearbulk Group, Switzerland. Previous positions include CFO of Goldbach Group SIX Swiss Exchange, and Steiner Group. He also held various national and international financial positions within Swissair Group, after starting his career in corporate finance at Credit Suisse. He is an author, and lecturer at different educational institutions. Publications: *M&A: Erfolg dank Integrationsmanagement* (2015), *Der Fremdverkauf einer Familienunternehmung im Nachfolgeprozess. Motive—Vorgehenskonzept—Externe Unterstützung* (1995), *Bestellerkompetenz Facility Management. Strategie—Organisation—Prozesse* (2015).

Markus Braun has a Ph.D. in Economics and Head of International Business ABF at ZHAW University of Applied Sciences, School of Management and Law (Switzerland). He is a lecturer of business administration and also received a Ph.D. in Business Administration from the University of Basel (Switzerland). He was Head of Corporate Office at Diethelm Keller Holding AG in Zurich (Switzerland) from 2004 until 2013; prior to that, he held the position of Group CFO and Deputy CEO of Nuance Group in Zurich (Switzerland), and various national and international financial positions at Novartis/Ciba-Geigy. Markus studied business administration at the University of St. Gallen and economics at the University of Basel. He is a member of several advisory boards of science and economics. Publication: *M&A: Erfolg dank Integrationsmanagement* (2015), *Project Costs in Pharmaceutical Research & Development* (PhD thesis, 1987).

List of Figures

Fig. 1.1	Key success factors of the entire M&A process. Source: A.T. Kearney (1998) and Schreiner et al. (2010, p. 291)	3
Fig. 1.2	Details concerning M&A transactions that have been included in this research. Source: Bergamin/Braun	5
Fig. 1.3	Steps within the framework of an integration project. Source: Bergamin/Braun	6
Fig. 1.4	Five highly influential factors that can make or break an integration project. Source: Bergamin/Braun	24
Fig. 2.1	In sales and marketing, HR and IT, there is ample room for improvement in terms of integration ability. Source: Deutsch and West (2010, p. 8)	35
Fig. 2.2	In the course of integration, neuralgic points are transposed into a performance transformation concept. Source: Bergamin/Braun	36
Fig. 2.3	Performance transformation concept. Source: Bergamin/Braun	36
Fig. 2.4	Performance transformation concept—step 1. Source: Bergamin/Braun	37
Fig. 2.5	Organizing the chief integration office. Source: Bergamin/Braun	40
Fig. 2.6	Performance transformation concept—step 2. Source: Bergamin/Braun	42
Fig. 2.7	Individual performance transformation design. Source: Jansen and Brügger (2012, p. 665); see also: Schreiner et al. (2010, p. 302ff)	43
Fig. 2.8	Types of integration and rising demands on post-merger managements. Source: Jansen and Brügger (2012, p. 677); also see: Müller-Stewens, Konzeptionelle Entscheidungen (2010, p. 9), also see: Bucerius (2004, p. 14 ff.), also see: Hackmann (2011, p. 177 ff)	44
Fig. 2.9	Areas of integration. Source: Unger (2007, p. 878)	45
Fig. 2.10	Prioritization of integration measures. Source: Bergamin/Braun. See also: Müller-Stewens et al. (2012, p. 10)	48

Fig. 2.11	Performance transformation concept—step 3. Source: Bergamin/Braun	54
Fig. 2.12	Performance transformation concept—step 4. Source: Bergamin/Braun	57
Fig. 2.13	Performance transformation concept—step 5. Source: Bergamin/Braun	60
Fig. 2.14	Integration scorecard. Source: Bergamin/Braun, based on Müller-Stewens (2006, p. 16)	61
Fig. 3.1	Standard PMI organization at dormakaba. Source: Bergamin/Braun	77
Fig. 3.2	Conflict management during M&A transaction and integration phases. Source: Bergamin/Braun, and André Sutter from SeestattExperts	84
Fig. 3.3	RAPID® (is a registered trademark of Bain & Company, Inc.)—a methodology for decision making. Source: Bain & Company	85

List of Checklists

Checklist 1	Scaling and Standardization in an International Context.......	52
Checklist 2	Institutionalize Integration Office Responsibility................	64
Checklist 3	Enforce Performance Transformation............................	64
Checklist 4	Exploit Growth Dynamics...	65
Checklist 5	Take Care of Talents...	65
Checklist 6	Introduce Integration Monitoring................................	66

Integration Management in Mergers and Acquisitions: Success Factors and Pitfalls

1.1 Integration and Transformation Is Essential for the Success of an M&A Transaction

The transaction market is going full steam ahead again, following a fairly quiet recent past. Many companies have re-indicated their interest, and other companies as new prospective buyers have joined their ranks. Full war chests, low interest rates and currency impact have whetted a veritable appetite for acquisitions. Other influencing factors thereby are operational requirements, such as the expansion of a limited position in the home market, access to international procurement markets or the reaction to structural changes in the respective sectors.

Acquiring a company is a landmark decision that is fraught with risk. The preparations and implementation of an acquisition require extensive resources and specific skills. For this reason, Shell's acquisition of British BG Group or the merger of the Swiss locking systems company Kaba with the German Dorma to form a new industry leader, involves substantial amounts of financial and human resources.

Other recent examples such as the mergers of Holcim and Lafarge, or Sika and Saint Gobain, amply demonstrate that the challenges remain monumental. International transactions or the mergers of partners on an equal footing may markedly increase the complexity of such undertakings.

A merger or an acquisition—also referred to as M&A—comprises different phases: M&A initiation, reconciliation of interests, due diligence, contract preparation, contract closing, and integration. An acquisition generates opportunities. Opportunities should be maximized, risks minimized. The executive board of a company will strive to reach this goal by means of prudent and cautious preparation, a meticulous plan of action, and stringent, full enforcement thereof. An acquisition ensues significantly higher risks than any other entrepreneurial investments, such as for instance the development and introduction of new products.[1] For this reason, recent decades have witnessed a professionalization of M&A knowledge and competence. Considerable funds and time have been invested in the relevant training of both managements and specialists, and many companies are now familiar with the transaction-specific M&A techniques.[2]

Every M&A transaction has its idiosyncrasies and particular degree of complexity, all of which require specific competences far beyond the mere hard skills. In fact, soft skills are the decisive factors when it comes to dealing with other cultures or collaborating with equal partners. An M&A project becoming media knowledge, inevitably results in additional time pressure for the management to appropriately define their priorities. Many mergers and acquisitions demonstrate that the human factor plays a decisive role. As a result, managements must adamantly work towards an implementation of the targeted goals in collaboration with their new partners.

Operative focus, relentless cost pressure and high demands on leadership challenge a management in its plans to implement such extraordinary and complex projects. When it comes to M&A competence, small and medium-sized enterprises (SMEs) in particular are often lean and streamlined. They are challenged to increase the capacities required in order to cope with the tall order of an M&A transaction and target-aimed enforcement thereof. The high expectations that go hand in hand with the substantial amount to be invested in the acquisition of a company do not allow for failure.

However, in many cases the targeted goals and expectations cannot be met. Half of all M&A transactions are not successful and do not add value to the companies involved. According to several different studies, the initiation phase as well as the post-acquisition integration phase prove to be crucial to the success of a merger or an acquisition of a company. The transaction as such, however, thereby constitutes fewer risks for the success of an M&A project.[3] Other studies attribute the actual value added of a merger or acquisition to the integration phase, and they report the strategic and organizational congruousness of the companies involved to have less of an influence on the success of a project than generally assumed (Fig. 1.1).[4]

Müller-Stewens aptly describes this challenge: "After the legal papers are signed, the major task still lies ahead. The problem is to keep the faces smiling the morning after."[5] The integration phase is strongly influenced by feelings, and rational maxims of action are often put to the test. "The main challenge of integration is its complexity. Organizations are extremely sensitive during this time and act

---

[1]Müller-Stewens (2006, p. 3), Spill (2007, p. 1 f).
[2]Unger (2007, p. 876) (A.T. Kearney), Schreiner et al. (2010, p. 291), see also: Jansen and Brügger (2012, p. 663).
[3]Unger (2007, p. 876) (A.T. Kearney), Schreiner et al. (2010, p. 291).
[4]Jansen and Brügger (2012, p. 663).
[5]Müller-Stewens (2006, p. 3): "After the legal papers are signed, the major task still lies ahead. The problem is to keep the faces smiling the morning after."

1.1 Integration and Transformation Is Essential for the Success of an M&A Transaction

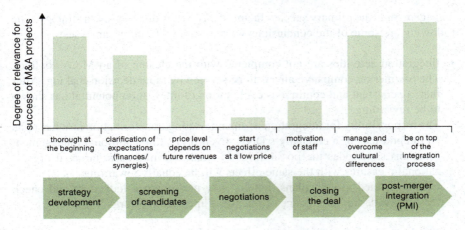

Fig. 1.1 Key success factors of the entire M&A process. Source: A.T. Kearney (1998) and Schreiner et al. (2010, p. 291)

on the basis of a general atmosphere that allows little prediction with respect to its development, and is rather difficult to influence."[6]

Our own experience has also shown that many M&A projects do not develop according to plan. In many cases, the opportunities that a merger or acquisition provides to advance a company are not fully exploited. Thereby, we have made the following observations:

- Company mergers and acquisitions are complex projects. Their successful implementation requires substantial resources, tact and intuition, and a bit of luck. It is not a run-of-the-mill transaction and those involved therefore may lack the skills for a professional execution of an M&A project.
- Lean organizations struggle to cope with mergers or company acquisitions. Required resources are not allocated in time.
- The management gets involved in the transaction, but then withdraws its involvement. As the integration process ceases to be the main focus, its implementation buckles under a lack of stringency and consequence.
- Strongly people-oriented companies do not follow a rigid plan of integration measures, but instead proceed situationally and in many cases even hesitantly.

Many companies subject to an M&A transaction fail to fully exploit the potential of a merger or acquisition, as they do not pay sufficient attention to the integration of the newly acquired company. We are adamant that a stringent integration

---

[6]Ibid.

management is the primary success factor of any M&A driven growth strategy. The following are some of the conclusions we have drawn from our analyses:

- Integration activities are not completed with the closing of an M&A contract. The pre-merger company value is to be secured by rapid decision-making. After that, a persistent and continuous exploitation of integration potential has shown to be rewarding.
- The responsibility for integration as an undeviating transformation task has to be an integral part of a company's DNA. Even if creating additional management functions supersedes the possibilities of small and mid-caps, targeted organizational measures with the same effects will be equally rewarding.
- Clearly-defined growth plans, binding key performance indicators and check lists underline the importance of relentless integration efforts.

This book is an account of our experiences of company mergers and acquisitions as well as the subsequent implementations of growth strategies. These experiences are the result of over 30 years in our capacities as chief financial officers (CFOs) of various private and publicly traded Swiss and international companies. Our observations are based on more than thirty accomplished M&A business transactions from different industries with an overall transaction value of more than CHF 2 billion. We were personally involved in responsible positions in all these transactions (Fig. 1.2).

We are focusing our attention on companies with a small to medium market capitalization, so-called small and mid-caps.[7] Small and mid-caps denote small and medium-sized enterprises with a market capitalization or company value of CHF 100 million to 2 billion—a segment that we know very well from our own experience. Based on our intimate knowledge of such medium-sized companies, we know from first-hand experience how these firms most struggle in their endeavors to grow. Unlike large-scale companies, they only ever have access to limited resources, and management decisions with respect to the enforcement of growth strategies may have a dramatic impact on their business performance. This book aims to support management personnel and practitioners in small and medium-sized enterprises that do not have specialized teams or divisions focusing on corporate finance, M&A and integration.

We have developed an easily applicable and practical manual that aims to support the management to optimize and streamline their growth strategy with the help of a persistent integration and transformation management. This book does not offer back seat advice but instead roots in our own experiences, successes and failures in which we were directly involved in our capacities as management personnel. Each individual M&A transaction has been assessed from an inside

---

[7]We distinguish this category from large companies that—in Switzerland for instance—are largely represented in the Swiss Market Index (SMI).

1.1 Integration and Transformation Is Essential for the Success of an M&A Transaction

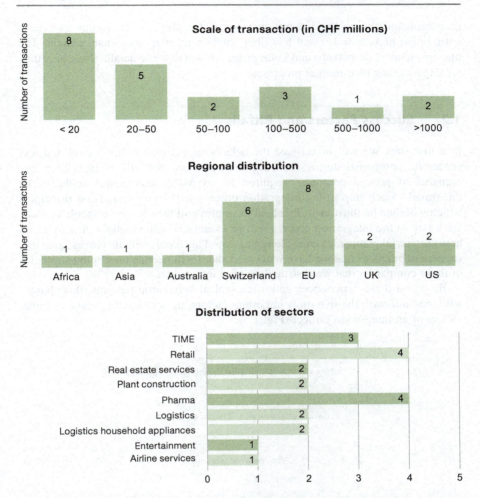

Fig. 1.2 Details concerning M&A transactions that have been included in this research. Source: Bergamin/Braun

perspective taking into consideration the political environment, transaction dynamics and decision-making processes involved.

This book is also the result of many conversations with members of boards of directors and managements. Its purpose is to provide entrepreneurs, managers and members of the board—but also students of business economics and other interested readers—with practical advice on integration management. If beyond our declared goals, this publication manages to bridge a gap in academic business research, as science-orientated practitioners, we shall be pleased even more.

We will illustrate our experiences in three steps: This chapter will explore the key factors for success or failure of integration management in M&A projects. On this basis, Chap. 2 will formulate our recommendations with respect to performance transformation during the integration process. Chapter 3 will feature interviews with global players and reveal how they implement integration management. The managements of dormakaba and LafargeHolcim will disclose details about how they are experiencing their merger processes.

1.2 Success Factors and Pitfalls

In a first step, we will investigate the behavioral patterns of successful and less successful companies during the integration process. We will devise a best-case scenario of how a company acquired in an M&A transaction ought to be integrated.[8] Each step in the integration process will feature hands-on principles which will then be illustrated. Practical examples will thereby serve as role models. Each step in the integration process will be examined individually with a focus on how successful companies cope along the way. This report will also investigate less successful practices that we have witnessed and it will decode the coping strategies of those companies that were struggling with integration.

Based on these experiences and often typical behavioral patterns, this chapter will conclude with the five most important factors, in our view the make or break factors of an integration project (Fig. 1.3).

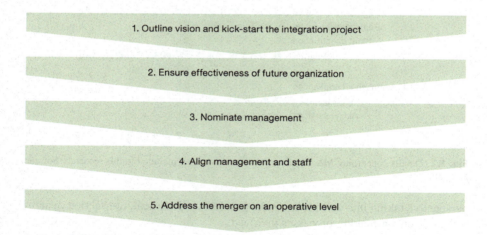

Fig. 1.3 Steps within the framework of an integration project. Source: Bergamin/Braun

---

[8]Gerds and Schewe have established an analogous line of action concept. In the following, this concept will be brought into question and be amended on the basis of our practical experience and a series of interviews.

1.3 Clearly Outline Your Vision and Organize the Integration Project

The closing of contract does not mark the completion of an M&A transaction. The closing and ensuing transfer of ownership in fact starts the important phase of the integration process. However, the integration process and its course of action ought to be outlined well ahead of the transaction.[9] Companies are well advised to identify those responsible of the integration process as well as configure their line of approach at an early stage.

1.3.1 Principles

1.3.1.1 Devise an Integration Plan at an Early Stage and Outline a Clear Vision

The early stages of an acquisition project are often characterized by an insufficient knowledge about the target organization—be it concerning its power and people issues, i.e. its personnel and organizational situation or the skills and competences in place. Despite this lack of detailed knowledge, early decision-making is the advisable course of action. This involves a clear outline of the vision with respect to an imminent acquisition. A clearly stated vision promotes a spirit of optimism and defines a goal. This in turn averts feelings of insecurity within the company itself and conveys a powerful image to the outside world. At this early stage, the importance of a vision is unquestionable. Equal weight must be given to hand-picked integration teams, and to the milestones that have to be set for the entire integration process. The 80:20 rule in the decision-making phase observes that a small number of decisions have a disproportionately great influence on the company. The application of this rule ensures that staff are not subjected to any lengthy periods of insecurity, and allows routine business operations to proceed unhampered.

1.3.1.2 Leading-Edge Enterprises Put Their Leaders First

Companies that have mastered an M&A transaction successfully—here referred to as leading-edge enterprises—further ensure that the appropriate people are involved in the integration project.[10] They hand pick their staff. The choice of a suitable candidate may focus on their in-depth business knowledge as well as their analytical and conceptual skills. These candidates must be approved and accepted in both organizations. Leading-edge enterprises insist that their promoters take part in the integration project. Promoters are firmly-established managerial or executive members of staff, and ideally involved in the acquisition decision. This early involvement warrants their motivation and commitment to the transaction.[11]

---

[9]Grube and Töpfer (2002, p. 104), Bertels and Cosach (2012, p. 535 f).
[10]Gerds and Schewe (2014, p. 152 ff).
[11]Grube and Töpfer (2002, p. 112).

Promoters in leading-edge enterprises also dedicate at least half of their working time to the integration project.

1.3.1.3 Involving the Corporate Management Is Important, but not Enough

Involving the corporate management is instrumental in tearing down integration barriers from the start. However, the hierarchical element alone decidedly lacks drive; savvy companies are advised to involve key personnel with solid operative skills into the project, with an excellent knowledge of the company's organizational structure.[12] The organization team must above all unconditionally commit to this project and keep each other in line.[13] Win hearts and minds.

1.3.1.4 Successful Companies Capitalize on Previous Integration Planning Experiences

Past experiences with company mergers influence integration success.[14] Thorough tried and tested integration planning is irremissible for each single integration project. Planning denotes a plan of action that establishes the principal working steps, milestones and persons in charge. Experienced managers know that reaching the ultimate goal may or may not be quite so straightforward. It is therefore crucial to pointedly depict various "what if" scenarios and prepare contingency plans.

The following focuses on three practical examples: the behavioral patterns of leading-edge enterprises and less successful protagonists with respect to company integration.

1.3.2 Success Factor: Stringent and Systematic Implementation Thanks to Coaching

> **Practical Example**
> An international logistics services company acquired a regional European aviation company. Albeit the acquisition as such was burdened with a number of challenges, the integration process was textbook. Representatives of the corporate management on the buyer's side took an active part in the integration project. At the same time, an experienced network specialist who was held in high esteem in the parent company and a young talent were taken on board for integration operations.
> The network specialist advised the local management on how to best integrate their regional network into international transport hubs. He devised a
>
> (continued)

---

[12]Gerds and Schewe (2014, p. 154).
[13]Grube and Töpfer (2002, p. 112).
[14]Gerds and Schewe (2014, p. 152).

1.3 Clearly Outline Your Vision and Organize the Integration Project

> sustainable operating plan and supported the local management in their discussions about their course of action in dealing with the corporation. As an integral part of the local management, the network manager at the same time acted as a gateway to the newly appointed corporate management. The young talent on the other hand assumed the task of head of controlling and was responsible for integrating the financial management of the acquired aviation company into that of the merged company. He was also a member of the team that supported the post-merger integration of the company. The team was mentored and moderated by an external strategy consultant.

The integration project above demonstrates the benefits of tailored consulting and monitoring in a complex, multicultural environment. Talents of the acquiring and acquired organization join forces and are supported by external consultants.[15] This turns those affected into protagonists that become part of the integration process. Open communication makes for a commonly assessable and transparent process. The corporate management stipulates the integration goals, the integration team consists of equal members who communicate openly and independently of their allegiances to either the acquiring or acquired organization. Conflicts can be resolved by integrating all options and perspectives into the equation and by addressing feelings of friction and resistance from the start.

1.3.3 Pitfall: Integration Manager with the Right Pedigree, but not from the Same Stable

According to Gerds/Schewe,[16] companies with successful M&A credentials distinguish themselves because they involve promoters into their integration team. Our practical examples demonstrate that this principle is often neglected, as the following typical constellations display:

The corporate management in many cases closely monitored the initiation and transaction phases. However, when the transaction was closed, the acquisition ceased to be the management's main concern, and integration tasks were largely delegated. When integration challenges became apparent, the corporate management generally remained unconcerned.

The integration manager is the be-all and end-all of an integration project. Practice shows that designating the person in charge of integration is imperative, but their appointment alone will not suffice.

---

[15]Böning (2010, p. 355 f).
[16]Gerds and Schewe (2014, p. 152).

> **Practical Example**
> In the course of an acquisition, a fast-growing corporation in the TIME sector (telecommunications, information, media and entertainment) recruited an external integration manager with ample management experience from comparable positions, the pertinent industry knowledge, and business experience in the relevant local markets. As an external, however, he was not part of the team of promoters. He was in charge of enforcing landmark integration decisions that had been made by a third party. Soon, the integration project started to buckle under the strain and spiraled out of control. Amongst other things, the crisis revealed an urgent need for extensive restructuring, which utterly overran the local management. The integration manager suggested radical changes that only met the local management's disapproval. Ultimately, the chief executive of the corporation took sides with the local management; the integration responsible was soon left stranded, morphed into the general scapegoat, and consequently failed in all his endeavors. Had the integration manager been recruited amongst the team of promoters, those in charge of the acquisition might have felt more responsible to enforce the proposed measures.

The following is an example of similarly pear-shaped integration efforts. In his case, the integration manager was not a member of the acquiring organization, but instead had been employed ad interim for this particular acquisition project. Involvements on an interim basis may be perfectly valuable. In this particular case, however, this solution proved to be rather problematic, as the integration manager was not a member of the team of promoters. The integration project was encumbered with a number of issues right from the start. The management delegated all integration duties and declared the ad interim manager responsible for the ensuing failure of the project.

1.3.4 Pitfall: Side Plots Are Distracting

Devising an integration plan and its official approval creates transparency in an already complex integration process. It combines clear priorities with milestones and ensuing responsibilities.

> **Practical Example**
> The increase of digital value adding activities, in particular the challenge to maximize the benefits of modern information and communication technologies, is driving a corporation to acquire a majority share of a publicly traded corporation in a bidding process. The acquired company plays a leading role in the digital business models of its segment. According to the prevailing
>
> (continued)

company law, which applies to this transaction, the acquiring corporation is entitled to a squeeze-out of minority shareholders and an ensuing going private upon payout of an appropriate compensation payment. The main shareholder puts in a request with the competent judge to appoint an external auditor, who in turn needs to assess the adequacy of the compensation payment.

Minority shareholders may requisition the court to assess the height of their compensation payment by process of elimination. The so-called mediation procedure aims to avoid any delays of the implementation of structural measures under corporate law. Any disagreement on the amount of the compensation and the degree of efficacy of the structural measures applied are treated as two entirely different matters. This safeguards the interests of both sides: minority shareholders are guaranteed an appropriate price, main shareholders are assured a speedy transaction without further ado.

The exclusion of minority shareholders and the subsequent mediation procedure, however, in this particular case resulted in a delay of the integration process and hindered its systematic and comprehensive enforcement. Buyers were unsure whether drastic management changes, products and processes prior to the legal procedures would be at all feasible, and feared a too radical course of action to have a detrimental effect on the mediation procedure. In the wake of all this uncertainty, time was ticking away until the necessary changes in company structure were finally undertaken. The delay of this transaction stalled its drive, and when the turnover development under the old management of the target organization failed to meet expectations, the management shuffled off any responsibility to the acquiring organization. They blamed integration efforts to have negatively influenced their work climate and irrevocably damaged their market reputation. The old management did not leave the company until the final transaction fee for the minority shareholders had been established. The company eventually underwent a drastic change in strategy, albeit with considerable delay.

With the benefit of hindsight, it became evident that conscious integration efforts could have been made as early as during the elimination procedure of the minority shareholders. A systematic course of action and a thick skin against the intimidation tactics of the target organization are more than likely to have produced better results. The acquiring organization got distracted in a maze of irrelevancy and side plots. Behavioral economist and Nobel Prize laureate, Daniel Kahneman refers to this phenomenon as "availability cascade",[17] a self-reinforcing cycle and set of distorted reactions to risks that often leads to inadequate prioritization of problems and challenges. In other words: A relatively minor incident, such as the intimidation

---

[17]Kahneman (2012, p. 178 ff).

tactics of the target organization in the example above, leads to debilitating beliefs that in turn culminate in an inadequate order of priorities.

> **Bottom Line**
>
>
>
> - *Integration planning has to be finalized before the closing of an M&A transaction.*
> - *Only the best take over as promoters of the integration project.*
> - *The project vision has to be clearly communicated from the word go, and key positions and milestones have to be set.*
>
> *Result*:
>
> – *Integration planning considerably curbs feelings of insecurity that may arise amongst employees.*
> – *A clear vision denotes a clear line of action, fosters a team spirit and conveys a powerful image to the outside world.*
>
>
>
> - *Integration endeavors are neglected in the face of other priorities.*
> - *The overall integration management responsibility is delegated to staff employees.*

1.4 Secure the Future Organization's Efficacy

Following a merger or acquisition, the new company has to resume its business as usual as quickly as possible. In order to secure smooth operations, the two organizations have to properly merge and focus their exploitation of synergies on genuine value drivers.[18]

1.4.1 Principles

1.4.1.1 Leading-Edge Companies Will not Content Themselves with Mere "Docking"

Integration is about determining management and organizational structures of the newly created union. Thereby, the distribution of competences between

---

[18]Bertels and Cosach (2012, p. 542 f).

headquarter and the local entity is essential. Leading-edge enterprises do not content themselves with "soft integration"[19] or mere "docking", just because purely political reasons or a decentralized management philosophy might urge them to do so.[20] There are of course financial investments, such e.g. the involvement of Novartis in Roche or Toshiba's takeover of Landis & Gyr (the Swiss pioneers of smart meter and grid solutions) that are not driven by an approximation agenda. This above all has to be a conscious and situational decision.

1.4.1.2 Secure Business Operations and Highlight Additional Potential

In many cases, an organization's performance capability suffers during the integration phase.[21] That is why existing goals and budgets need to be re-iterated. However, cementing the status quo by no means suffices and will fall short of adding any value from a merger or acquisition. At the same time, a viable synergy potential has to be identified and articulated and broken down to the respective organizational entities by means of pro forma budgets and mid-term planning. Successful M&A companies define a binding and target-oriented course of action which is stated in their reporting. This is how they manage to focus on synergy potential and align it with both their management and the required resources. Not only do they target cost synergies, but they also distinguish themselves by means of their unmistakable drive for growth. Growth-oriented targeted revenues are largely responsible for the fact that both organizations shift their focus from self-obsession to the market and their clients. Both buyer and target organization should be delighted to forge and communicate their common future and business targets. This can only be done if there is room enough for maneuver.

1.4.1.3 Leading-Edge Enterprises Quickly Create Transparency

When it comes to key performance indicators, transparency is a must, not only in everyday operations but also with integration projects. Professional reporting is indispensable to keep shareholders in the loop, to review progress, and to provide situational planning requirements.[22] Immediate transparency yields quick results: genuine problems are identified and addressed head-on.

---

[19]Schreiner et al. (2010, p. 312 f).
[20]Gerds and Schewe (2014, p. 135 f).
[21]Grube and Töpfer (2002, p. 117).
[22]Gerds and Schewe (2014, p. 129).

The following two practical cases demonstrate these principles.

1.4.2 Success Factor: Utilize Growth and Knowledge Synergies

Careful analysis of possible synergies and a focus on a consolidated growth strategy may be rewarding for the integration process and those involved alike, as the following example shows.

> **Practical Example**
> A weighty real-estate service provider acquired a foreign European competitor. It was considerably smaller than the parent company, and focused on a specific real estate segment, i.e. real estate development. The responsible managers were quick to realize that over the years, the acquired company had forged an amazingly lucrative business model thanks to its outstanding real estate specialists. They excelled in the market due to their investment techniques. Despite their limited funds, they managed to realize sizeable real estate projects based on their sophisticated financing models in collaboration with third party providers. This specialized knowledge was fused with the parent company in the course of the integration process. The successful enforcement of respective financing models in various countries combined with the help of third party investors raised their equity base by a remarkable CHF 100 million. This allowed for the funding of an annually recurring investment volume of CHF 300 million.

This synergy potential was quantified by means of a business plan in the run-up to the transaction, and was finally approved in a consensus process between buyer and acquired company. The participatory approach i.e. to quantify financial goals and synergies was why the company's achievement of objectives never became a bone of contention.

1.4.3 Pitfall: Lack of Transparency for a Prolonged Period of Time

A frequent problem during the integration process of an acquired company is that the parent company communicates inadequately and lacks transparency. The following case amply documents this issue.

Practical Example
A large Swiss energy service provider and subsidiary of an international industrial conglomerate acquired a Swiss provider of renewable energy generation solutions. This transaction was a pure intragroup switchover as the Swiss target company had been under the wings of the industrial conglomerate's European division long before it was finally taken over by its Swiss subsidiary. The Swiss hailed this acquisition as a welcome expansion of their service provider portfolios and a boost to their market presence. In the run-up to the deal, due diligence was conducted rather sketchily, as the main focus seemed to be on a quick takeover more than anything else. The underlying assumption was that the target company was a flourishing enterprise that kept to corporation standards and therefore did not sport any noteworthy problems. The Swiss management made short process of the matter and integration was addressed locally and without any major assistance from the Swiss headquarter. For the existing management in the target organization this meant business as usual, and for a while they kept operating in the black. However, the cracks began to show in a series of projects. There was an increase in customer complaints, and headquarter noted a deterioration of the acquired company's liquidity situation. Soon, the parent company had to raise its credit to a company that was burning its candle at both ends. And this finally alerted headquarter to its plight.

Pundits of the project trade are familiar with the loopholes in the various accounting standards that allow for a rather flexible rendering of project results. The international accounting standard (IAS 11), which applies to the project business, determines that revenue recognition is based on the project review until the date when the project is completed, the net profit or loss for the period is to be calculated according to project stage. Hence, the threat remains that project leaders may render an unrealistic picture of a project's risks to boost its assessment, despite the need for a downgrade. As a result, the respective company will show an exaggerated profit. A decrease in or lack of project liquidity often point to flaws in a project.

This very situation applies to the acquired provider of renewable energy generation solutions mentioned above. The existing management failed to communicate project risks, and consistently good results did not raise suspicions with the parent company. Months later, liquidity problems prompted the headquarter management to review the project portfolio. It became evident that many projects in actual fact yielded negative results and that they were besieged with major risks. Headquarter had been too aloof for too long. The acquired company turned out to be the source of giant losses, many project managers left the company, and the company's local reputation nosedived. The parent company saw itself flung into restructure. The crisis in the acquired company had a detrimental effect on the entire corporation and destabilized it substantially.

> **Bottom Line**
>
>
>
> - Business operations are secured and friction loss is avoided.
> - The company concentrates on the genuine value adding drivers, and taps the respective synergy potential without delay.
> - The synergy potential and transparent reporting thereof become an integral part of the official management agenda, and its full exploitation is closely monitored.
>
> Result:
>
> – The company focuses on the value drivers and exploits any value adding potential.
> – The commitment and motivation to exploit synergies adds value.
>
>
>
> - Strategists establish the synergy potential without the responsible management's approval.
> - Core business is neglected as a result of the integration processes.

1.5 Appoint the Management Team

Rapid appointment of the new company management is of the essence. Ideally, the new top management is appointed from day one of the acquisition, at the latest, however, a hundred days after the deal is announced.[23]

Whatever the case, best practice is to eradicate any insecurities that may arise by obscure management conditions from the start, because they are often the source of problems during the integration process.

1.5.1 Principles

1.5.1.1 Appoint Top Management and Operative Management

The appointment of the operative management and composition of the new corporate management are relevant in equal measure. Most companies with an average performance only go as far as to re-organize their top management. Companies with successful M&A transactions distinguish themselves by their focus on an operative level and its personnel.

---

[23]Picot, Personelle Integration (2012a, b, p. 611).

This way, integration does not degenerate into a paper tiger, but instead leads to a transformation of operative structures within the framework of the new guidelines. The top management has the decisive vote in all fundamental decisions, but otherwise remains in the background. The necessary processes of change, on the other hand, are down to the operative management.[24] Regrettably, however, this is an exception to the rule.

1.5.1.2 Dispatch Operative Key Figures into Both Directions

When managers of the acquired company transfer to their parent company—or vice versa—both managements begin to interlock. Targeted redeployments indicate and herald cultural exchange, which instigates a transfer of knowledge between the two companies at the same time.[25]

1.5.1.3 Leading-Edge Enterprises Keep Key Employees Loyal to the Company over the Long Run

In unsettling times of change it is vital to keep key employees loyal to the company. Empirical studies,[26] however, document that in very many cases, up to 50% of all corporate management staff leave the company within the 2 years following the deal. Remuneration models as well as interesting career prospects and attractive projects undoubtedly raise a company's appeal and keep employees loyal. At the same time, employees with a consistently negative attitude towards the merger cannot be tolerated.[27]

1.5.2 Success Factor: A Holistic Approach

> **Practical Example**
> A large company for airline ground services—with a track record of company acquisitions—created a central corporate management pool with staff to be deployed to newly acquired companies. Ground handling services have a strong local orientation and their regional networks are of utmost importance. For this reason, most of the top managers were reconfirmed in their positions. They were local figureheads and provided the required contacts. The board of directors deployed its hand-picked corporate management staff to the newly acquired company in an effort to support the executives of the existing top management. Careful attention was given to a good mix and equal distribution of representatives of both the corporation and local company. This kind of human resources policy ensured that the required knowledge was soon

(continued)

---

[24]Gerds and Schewe (2014, p. 116).

[25]Gerds and Schewe (2014, p. 142), Picot, Personelle Integration (2012a, b, p. 613 f.).

[26]Picot, Personelle Integration (2012a, b, p. 606 f.).

[27]Gerds and Schewe (2014, 92 ff.), Grube and Töpfer (2002, p. 113).

circulating in the entire organization, and corporation-related standards were implemented wherever required. The deployment of open-minded and cooperative managers also transfused the parent company's culture to the operative level of the acquired company, and generated an intense exchange of knowledge and experience.

1.5.3 Pitfall: Top Management Keep Themselves to Themselves

If personnel changes only occur in the corporate management, integration becomes sluggish and substantially more difficult. We have observed many M&A transactions during which the operative level was neither subject to changes in personnel nor was there ever an informal exchange. The taken over subsidiaries maintained their complete autonomy, which in turn nipped any mutual learning processes in the bud. Potential synergies of the acquisition were not exploited, it remained but a geographical extension. The parent company acted as the controlling intermediary, integration, however, remained largely superficial.

Bottom Line

- *Immediate appointment of operative management safeguards the integration process.*
- *Deliberate deployment of cooperative management of the acquiring company to the target company—and vice versa—forges a close partnership and promotes an exchange of knowledge.*
- *Attractive remuneration schemes and key project assignments can secure staff loyalty.*

Result:

– *Handpicking management staff that are to be deployed to the emerging organization hails a new era.*
– *Bloodletting of key management staff—which in the worst case may make or break an integration project—can therefore be avoided.*

- *Management positions are staffed hesitantly and without conviction.*
- *The interests and needs of key employees are not taken seriously.*

1.6 One Team, One Goal

Mergers and acquisitions of companies present a challenge to all those involved in terms of adaptability and the will to change existing behavioral patterns and structures. For staff to sustainably change their habits and modus operandi, the intentions and goals of integration have to be reiterated over and over again. Communication gaps are to be avoided by all means. Insufficient communication breeds feelings of insecurity amongst staff, and spearheads any desire for change.[28]

1.6.1 Principles

1.6.1.1 Savvy and Successful Acquirers Train Their Staff
Companies that master a merger successfully not only communicate excellently and without gaps, but they also devote considerable time and effort to the training of their staff in order to bring their employees up to speed with the challenges ahead. Additional training is often required, because employees are overtaxed with integration-specific challenges, or because they simply do not master the necessary hard skills yet.[29]

1.6.1.2 Leading-Edge Companies Adapt and Orient Incentive Schemes to Their Target
A company can only be integrated successfully, if its integration efforts are backed by its employees. At the same time, transparent rules of the game must be communicated at an early stage. Leading-edge enterprises reward those members of staff who support the integration process. Respective incentives should be adequate so that employees can meet the set targets and genuinely embrace the challenges that come with integration. Including integration-specific goals in the yearly agreement on objectives for management and employees has also revealed to be particularly effective.[30]

1.6.2 Success Factor: Prolonged Initiation Phase

A well thought-through initiation phase to work out a plan with options and with quantified objectives yields substantial benefits in entering the mission-critical integration phase.

---

[28] Grube and Töpfer (2002, p. 112).
[29] Gerds and Schewe (2014, p. 175 ff).
[30] Gerds and Schewe (2014, p. 174 f).

> **Practical Example**
> A large Swiss infrastructure corporation entertained an amicable exchange with a foreign company in the same line of business locally. This exchange eventually led to a joint venture. The Swiss organization had a share of 49% in the mutual company, there was no need to consolidate it. It was not until years later that both partners decided to fully merge. Due diligence of the company they wanted to acquire was initiated to screen it for risks and to assess it, as particularly in the infrastructure line of business, any future success of a company relies on individual projects. This due diligence was conducted over an entire year. A third party—an M&A specialist—was consulted, and each and every project was analyzed meticulously and brought up to scratch. This thoroughness created a solid basis for the assessment and final takeover decision. The ensuing business plans served as a roadmap. Such a long initiation phase positively affected the key persons, because it provided them with ample time to get to know each other and build trust. They developed an understanding for the culture of the other party and gradually realized that a merger would be beneficial to all.[31] During due diligence, the target organization was made familiar with the most significant management tools of the parent company, notably the new International Financing Reporting Standards (IFRS), project-related controlling instruments, as well as risk management techniques. The staff involved could therefore benefit from a good few months to develop the respective skills.

1.6.3 Pitfall: Incentive Systems Gradually Lose Their Appeal

Tailored incentive systems and staff loyalty programs influence manager behavior.[32] Corporation-wide incentive systems, however, in many cases are unsuitable and not applicable for a particular company or business unit and the situation they find themselves in.

> **Practical Example**
> The unsuitability of incentive systems mentioned in the example above particularly applies to the following case: a growth company in the German-speaking world with a professionally managed and profitable organization on whose platform the company made acquisitions abroad. This off-shore part was in the early stages of development and still undergoing intense processes of change. The incentive system focused on individual business units. As a
>
> (continued)

---

[31] See also Schreiner et al. (2010, p. 303).
[32] Jansen and Brügger (2012, p. 689 f).

result, the managers of the profitable units reveled in generous bonuses. The off-shore managers on the other hand, had drawn the short straw: they were only awarded minimal bonus compensations because of the unsatisfactory results of their units. Unjustly so, as their assignments had been considerably more challenging and of vital importance for the development of the entire corporation. This incentive system grew a rift in the corporation: The management of the profitable core business unit remained unaffected by the sluggish development of the off-shore activities and hence saw no need to support their colleagues. The key figures in charge of implementing the growth strategy were not rewarded for their efforts; on the contrary, they were financially disadvantaged and put their careers on the line, as there was no staff loyalty program. The only group of people in the offshore unit to benefit from a positive business development were the managers of the acquired company. During the transition time they were rewarded earn-out payments that depended on the company's revenues.

Bottom Line

- *The top management must communicate at regular intervals in order to induce change in staff behavior.*
- *Employee events and training are indispensable tools for promoting the new strategic course of action.*

Result:

- *A new company spirit emerges and people perceive integration and the change it brings as reasonable and important.*

- *Employees are not or only inadequately informed about the integration efforts and therefore take a passive stance.*
- *Employees do not know how they or their immediate environment could possibly benefit from the integration project.*

1.7 Join Forces on an Operative Level

Once all the preliminary parameters of a new organization have been set—i.e. its vision, integration plan, value drivers and key persons—the ensuing course of action requires meticulous planning. First, the pillars of integration are defined; the next step tackles the question of how the operative level can join forces.[33]

1.7.1 Principles

1.7.1.1 Integration Projects: A Chance to Improve Operative Processes
Leading-edge enterprises support their operative management effectively and do not leave integration success on an operative level to chance. An integration project is often accompanied by a seismic shift. Companies that conclude an M&A transaction successfully, grab this opportunity to enforce specific changes. This is particularly the case with parallel organizations, exaggerated centralization, too many hierarchy levels, bottle necks, hazy decision-making and legacy issues, which all may or may not be related to the integration project altogether.[34]

1.7.1.2 IT Is a Powerful Tool for Operative Amalgamation
Shared IT systems may support and promote an organization's efficiency to all intents and purposes. Depending on the situation, existing IT systems are retained or adapted selectively. In extreme cases, all the systems are migrated to a single common system.[35]

1.7.1.3 Leading-Edge Enterprises Do not Consolidate Operative Units at all Cost
Integration is not a run-of-the-mill project, and companies cannot be measured by the same yardstick. Individual constellations need to flow into the equation, and actions need to be tailored to the deal. If an acquired company's finances and entrepreneurial state are in dire straits, a two-staged course of action often applies: In a first step, the company is restructured and its health restored. In a second step, the organizations involved can proceed with their amalgamation.[36]

1.7.2 Success Factor: Amalgamation, but not at All Cost

Albeit operative interlocking and amalgamation of the different organizations is material, efforts have to remain within proportion. Only a meticulous analysis of

---

[33]Bertels and Cosach (2012, p. 547).
[34]Ibid., p. 541 f., Gerds and Schwebe (2014, p. 135).
[35]Gerds and Schewe (2014, p. 135).
[36]Ibid., p. 135 ff.

what can be standardized or unified and what not will produce the desired results. Real estate, for instance, is a predominantly local business.

For this reason, synergies that emerge for customer services of key accounts are mostly unrewarding. Collaborations in this field are a futile gamble with time and energy that only delivers disappointing results. If production and sales are largely local and there are hardly any points of contact with the corporation, IT consolidation may make little sense. Adhering to this principle proved to be game-changing in several of our practical examples. Managements consciously decided against standardizing certain processes but instead opted for autonomy and an independent modus operandi in selected subject areas. This course of action kept the entrepreneurial flame burning in their local units and motivated their staff to fight for the goals of the corporation.

1.7.3 Pitfall: Focus on Technical Details

Under the watchful eye of management experts, a weighty real estate corporation acquired a real estate management company. The integration plan or roadmap was ambitious and its schedule tight. They had also decided to impose new IT solutions for real estate management in an attempt to create a corporation-wide uniform IT system. Albeit enforcing this new IT solution was of relevance, it was not time-critical. And yet, this plan was enforced alongside all integration efforts. As a result, tackling all these tasks simultaneously soon became too complex and a strain. It thwarted the project and with it all the remaining integration measures.

> **Bottom Line**
>
>
>
> - *Integration of two organizations must include the operative level.*
> - *An integration project is an opportunity for change. It is an elegant way of revisiting delayed and overdue decisions.*
> - *Any IT synergy potential must be exploited, wherever useful.*
>
>   *Result:*
>
> - *The process of change on an operative level will not lack direction, but instead be systematic and effective.*
>
>
>
> - *Integration efforts are a matter of common sense; overzealous activism may soon meet with resistance.*

1.8 Key Factors of Integration Management

The practical examples we have examined reveal a particular, repeating pattern that was responsible for the success or failure of an integration project.[37] In other words, there are typical, recurring aspects that decidedly influence integration success. We shall refrain from statistical analysis of the collected data, practice itself, however, allows us to identify these key factors.

The analysis of our practical examples produces five factors with a major influence that will make or break an integration project: the organization and its leadership personalities, the degree of synergy exploitation, mobilization, resources and the integration project management.

The following focuses on these five factors (Fig. 1.4):

1.8.1 Organization and Leadership Personalities

Strong leadership figures exert a dominant influence on a company due to their charisma and leadership philosophy—particularly with strategic projects, e.g. acquisitions. For this reason, M&A projects in family-run businesses are sometimes different from non-family-run enterprises. Whereas family-specific characteristics are to be taken into account during the strategic and implementation

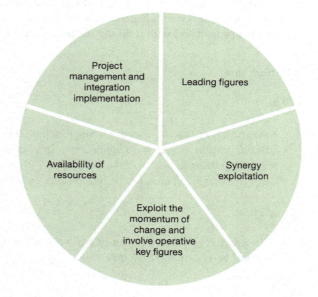

Fig. 1.4 Five highly influential factors that can make or break an integration project. Source: Bergamin/Braun

---

[37]Cf. analogous empirical results in: Schreiner et al. (2010, p. 313).

phases, the object identification and transaction phases are largely independent of company type.[38]

In organizations that are strongly influenced by one person, this omnipresence is striking; the company aligns itself thoroughly with its charismatic leader. In such organizations, products and services are often tightly connected with their influential figureheads. All going well, a charismatic company leader can support their management team to achieve integration success. A difficult staff constellation, on the other hand, may airbrush out economic principles during integration. Those in charge determine the course of action, resistance or opposing views are ignored. In such an environment and with these specific risks, companies are advised to undergo a slow integration phase that meets with wide support in the target company.[39]

When it comes to assessing the success of an integration project, empirical studies[40] establish a glaring discrepancy between self-image and public image. Whereas the management will praise their integration project as a success, the assessment of those who were not directly involved may be entirely different. It is a phenomenon that we have often witnessed in connection with charismatic leaders. They are either in outright denial about problems or they fail to take them seriously.

It is empirically debatable what influence companies' intense acquisition activity actually has on successful integration.[41] Organizations that steadily grow thanks to their M&A transactions, ordinarily have a tried and tested integration management. They have learnt from past mistakes. Our practical examples show that strong management personalities can capitalize on this knowledge, or they can disregard it. Their position of power allows them to influence the composition of their management teams. In the worst case, they lack any acquisition experience and fail to compensate for this disadvantage by consulting the appropriate management staff.

Several practical cases document the benefits of a project in which those in charge of the acquisition decision also take a vital role in the integration process, ideally as promoters. The smart course of action is to assign a representative of the management to the integration team, a person who is firmly established in the parent organization and fully supports the acquisition decision. Having witnessed both due diligence and the acquisition negotiations, this person bears a wealth of information and warrants the implementation of the management's preliminary targets. This staff constellation secures a company's commitment to successful integration. Failure would be a double blow. Practice has often demonstrated how the top management orchestrated a takeover and used the acquisition as a marketing platform. With the contract closing, all integration efforts were delegated altogether—in the worst case to people outside the circle of promoters. If integration did not go according to plan, the "consultants" or "newcomers" were easy to blame.

---

[38] Raffel (2006, p. 119), Schäfer and Blankenberg (1997, p. 1 ff).
[39] Fuhrer (2007, p. 236 f).
[40] Spill (2007, p. 16 f).
[41] Jansen and Brügger (2012, p. 691 f.), Müller-Stewens et al. (2010, p. 207 f.), and Unger (2007, p. 875).

If the target organization is run by its owner, and if the owner remains the chief executive after its sale, integration may become troublesome.[42] Various practical cases demonstrate that integration processes can be particularly challenging against the background of such a management constellation. For a successful small and mid-cap entrepreneur to be assigned a managerial position within a corporation is a seismic shift. The person was used to taking decisions autonomously and to enforcing them single-handedly. She or he decided on the strategy, the structure and processes in their company and they supervised the operative business. Within the framework of a cooperation, superordinate management targets play a substantial role, and the former company owner's autonomy is inevitably stunted. Many management personalities struggle to subordinate to such corporation-wide rules, which has a detrimental effect on a company's integration. Many times in such cases, there are so-called earn-out agreements that concede earn-out payments to the seller. The amount of such payments depends on the company's future result. This ensures that seller and chief executive continue to be motivated to meet their financial targets; however, there is no guarantee that the seller will support the integration process. Analogous importance is attached to the so-called "sacred cows", i.e. the key persons in the acquired company. Their privileged position is a result of political circumstances. In these cases, it remains to be seen for how long their position will be tolerated, and whether it would not be wiser to part with them for the benefit of the process of change.

Financial due diligence is a must when it comes to mergers and acquisitions. But who will also conduct due diligence when it comes to their own company culture? Who will take a closer look at existing management and leadership skills? Management audit—i.e. rating the performance of managerial staff—can be a useful tool in disclosing such aspects. Those refusing to deal with such matters, must be conscious of the risk this decision implies.[43]

1.8.2 Exploit Synergies

The way in which synergy exploitation is tackled during an integration process will decisively influence the success or failure of a project.

The discussion about synergies is often associated with the topic of costs. Significant synergy achievements are not only the result of cost cuts, but they are also attained via the development of new markets, additional revenue potential, and the transfer of new knowledge. These market-specific synergies in particular have a huge impact on the integration outcome. Experts insist that growth is a prerequisite if new value is to be generated.[44] Problems during takeover often lead to

---

[42]Böning (2010, p. 352).
[43]Böning (2010, p. 357).
[44]Jansen and Brügger (2012, p. 688 f.), Müller-Stewens et al. (2010, p. 219), Rothenbücher et al. (2012, p. 6), and Unger (2007, p. 874).

introversion, turns a blind eye to the outside world and the future, and hampers innovations.[45] It is certainly helpful to define a clear integration target figure by calculating synergy potentials as early as during due diligence and the assessment.[46]

In this respect, examples such as the following are eminent and encouraging success stories: The acquisition of a Turkish airline service company provided the buying organization with an interesting market expansion of their traditional business. The acquisition at the same time presented an opportunity to sell other products from the parent company's portfolio by cross-selling via their new platform.[47] In another case, the financial know-how of the target company could be multiplied in the corporation. The learning process between buyer and seller yielded positive results for both.

Finding the right balance is key when it comes to synergy exploitation. Synergies may be wasted when organizations are merely lined up next to one another. Over-exploitation of synergies may, however, result in friction between or among companies.

A symbiotic integration architecture is successful in many cases. Symbiotic integration applies where autonomy can partially be retained and mutual dependencies can be put to use at the same time. The benefits of such a model are that in the case of a decentralized integration architecture, pending matters are not delayed further. The top management, on the other hand, is not overstrained within the framework of a centralized architecture.[48]

In some practical cases, synergies could not be exploited fully and if, only hesitantly. A slack approach in implementing the integration timetable or roadmap, reservations or political calculation meant that synergy potentials could not be accessed; or possible synergies were recognized but not enforced until much later.

1.8.3 Put Mobilization to Use

The takeover of a company is a growth initiative that ensues challenging changes in an organization's structure and leadership. Exploiting the momentum of such a change is decisive for the creation of value of growth companies.[49] An integration project's changes ripple through its immediate environment. Its more distant environment—the entire corporation—can exploit a takeover to target changes, e.g. to resolve long-standing problems of legacy issues.[50] This takeover momentum entails golden opportunities. Integration is a matter of a small circle, only the

---

[45]Jansen and Brügger (2012, p. 690 f).
[46]Unger (2007, p. 887).
[47]Rothenbücher et al. (2012, p. 10).
[48]Jansen and Brügger (2012, p. 685).
[49]Rothenbücher et al. (2012, p. 7).
[50]Bertels and Cosach (2012, p. 541 f).

management is involved, and operative key figures are excluded. Such a constellation can stifle the manifold impulses that are generated in the course of an acquisition. The resulting consequences are often not recognized or are not taken into account. What happens when the earn-out period ends, the top management of the acquired company have run off and no viable candidate from the company's own ranks has been groomed for the target organization?

Successful examples show that an acquisition project triggers a corporation-wide and strategically decisive process of change. A leading construction corporation—firmly established in the construction industry and operating as a general contractor—acquires a successful real estate developer in an abroad market. The acquisition is a success and the financial targets are fully met. There is an intense transfer of knowledge as well. The target company is welcomed into the corporation with open arms, which shifts the corporation's profile towards real estate development and real estate service provider. The acquisition therefore leads to a strategic realignment of the entire corporation.

1.8.4 Resources

Resources are a further key parameter that can make an integration process a success or failure. The merger of two companies often is a large-scale project that strongly absorbs the entire organization. Sufficient resources have to be available to allow the management the necessary time to take care of integration and all ensuing projects. The resource costs of the integration phase must flow into the assessment of the company that will be acquired, so as to avoid unpleasant surprises. In the name of transparency and harmony, integration costs have to be disclosed well ahead of integration.

A long and intense initiation phase may reveal to be beneficial for a company's integration.[51] It means the key persons will have ample time to gradually acquaint themselves with one another and learn to appreciate their different cultures.

Selected key persons ought to be allocated a time budget to fully dedicate themselves to the integration project and its implementation. Small and mid-caps in particular—where staff units and supporting functions are rather exceptional—need to provide sufficient resources.[52] Our practical examples clearly demonstrate the importance of the resources issue. In many cases, the lack of integration resources eventually overstrained an organization, which had a detrimental effect on related projects within the company as well. Generating additional resources often proved to be more cost efficient than the repercussions of a lack of resources, particularly when integration problems lead to a company's introversion and the focus on clients and innovations is neglected.[53]

---

[51]Müller-Stewens et al. (2010, p. 213 f).
[52]Gerds and Schewe (2014, p. 84 ff.), Raffel (2006, p. 121), and Unger (2007, p. 881).
[53]Jansen and Brügger (2012, p. 690 f).

1.8.5 Integration Management Means Project Management

The examined practical cases also outline the significance of a professional project management during the integration phase of an acquisition. Meticulous due diligence is crucial for a successful merger or acquisition; in fact, the due diligence phase denotes the target company's acid test. This phase also allows people to get to know the acquired company's culture and find some common ground. A business plan or company assessment, or other documents that are compiled during due diligence, may be a welcome radar system during the integration phase.

The integration timetable is another weighty managerial tool. We believe this roadmap to be a conditio sine qua non. Surprisingly in fact, however, only every fifth company will employ such an integration roadmap as a governance tool.[54] This is startling particularly as we know that a tight integration management is a critical control variable for the success of an integration[55]: goals, milestones, responsibilities and measurement parameters are determined early on to secure the project's success. Interfaces and inter-dependencies are pinpointed by means of an integration plan and are coordinated via a centralized project management. The resources employed should cover all areas in question. Adequate allocation of resources and quality thereof is pertinent. This includes any allocation of full-time resources from both companies. Decision boards should be implemented for good in order to secure a rapid and smooth course of action. The analyzed practical examples and additional research[56] reveal that a tight project management and strict adherence to the integration roadmap are indeed rewarding. Meticulous planning provides security and prompts acceptance within a company and among its staff.[57]

Our practical experience, however, confirms that an overly participatory collaboration with the different contact groups within an integration framework is not rewarding by any means, true to the saying that too many cooks spoil the broth. We can safely establish that a casual or slapdash integration management will not produce the desired integration results. In these unsuccessful cases, substantial synergy effects as envisaged in the business plan were either not realized at all or too late. The persons in charge soon turned their backs on the milestones that were targeted by the business plan. Integration was slow, as the management was aiming to please all the parties involved and ultimately shied away from making decisions.[58] In the event of counter pressure from the acquired company's side, the integration plan was soon deviated from. Other significant projects within the corporation or mere side plots brought a distraction from all integration efforts. The integration roadmap was not imposed stringently and the target company was kept on a long leash for too long. The top management missed their change to create

---

[54]Unger (2007, p. 882).
[55]Neumann and Rumpf (1998, p. 4).
[56]Ungerath and Hoyningen-Huene (2005, p. 6).
[57]Müller-Stewens et al. (2010, p. 212 f.) and Böning (2010, p. 349).
[58]Böning (2010, p. 353 f).

transparency from the start.[59] This kind of conduct circumvented all the problems on hand initially, however, these issues soon resurfaced only to be more of an inconvenience than ever before.

1.8.6 The Most Important Points so Far

When it comes to integration, we regard the following factors as the stringent criteria for the success or failure of integration projects: leadership skills, synergy exploitation, mobilization, resources, and project management. Companies achieve better results in their integration management, if:

- Key leadership persons conduct the integration process in a positive way,
- Synergies are exploited persistently, but with a sense of proportion,
- The processes of change that are inherent to an integration project are employed actively,
- There are enough resources to be allocated,
- And integration efforts are implemented according to the guidelines of contemporary project management.

Individual integration projects doubtlessly play an important role in the creation of high performance organizations. Yet, there are a multitude of other forces outside the actual integration as such—e.g. leadership and company culture—that also influence a company's overall success.

The success of M&A projects might perhaps not reveal itself during integration, but much later. For this reason, high performance organizations distinguish themselves by means of their persistent pursuit of integration issues. The following will take a detailed look at this particular point.

The following chapter develops a practical manual of how professionals conduct integration management. Practical advice and checklists on every step of the way will assist you in implementing the desired measures.

References

Bertels, E., & Cosach, S. (2012). Integrationsmanagement. In G. Picot (Hrsg.), *Handbuch Mergers & Acquisitions: Planung – Durchführung – Integration* (5. Auflage). Stuttgart: Schäffer-Poeschel Verlag.

Böning, U. (2010). Übernahmen und Fusionen: Psychologie ist nicht alles – aber ohne Psychologie ist alles nichts. In G. Müller-Stewens, S. Kunisch, & A. Binder (Hrsg.), *Mergers & Acquisitions: Analysen, Trends und Best Practices*. Stuttgart: Schäffer-Poeschel Verlag.

---

[59]Rigall and Tarlaat (2010, p. 313): Empirical study on the success factors of integrations. Transparency from the start is a crucial factor for success.

References

Fuhrer, C. A. (2007). *Akquisitions- und Integrationsmanagement: Wie können Kompetenzen erfolgreich integriert und neuer Wertschöpfung zugeführt werden?* Dissertation, Hochschulschrift Universität St. Gallen.

Gerds, J., & Schewe, G. (2014). Post merger integration: Unternehmenserfolg durch integration excellence (5. Auflage). Berlin: Springer Verlag.

Grube, R., & Töpfer, A. (2002). *Post merger integration: Erfolgsfaktoren für das Zusammenwachsen von Unternehmen*. Stuttgart: Schäffer-Poeschel Verlag.

Jansen, S. A., & Brügger, C. (2012). Integrationsmanagement bei Unternehmenszusammenschlüssen. In G. Picot (Hrsg.), *Handbuch mergers and acquisitions: Planung – Durchführung – Integration* (5. Auflage). Stuttgart: Schäffer-Poeschel Verlag.

Kahneman, D. (2012). *Schnelles Denken, langsames Denken*. München: Siedler Verlag.

Kearney, A. T. (1998). Global PMI Survey.

Müller-Stewens, G. (2006). Konzeptionelle Entscheidungen beim Post-Merger-Management. In B. H. Wirtz (Hrsg.), *Handbuch Mergers & Acquisitions Management*. Wiesbaden: Gabler Verlag.

Müller-Stewens, G., Kunisch, S., & Binder, A. (Hrsg.) (2010). Mergers & Acquisitions: Analysen, Trends und Best Practices. Stuttgart: Schäffer-Poeschel Verlag.

Neumann, P., & Rumpf, B.-M. (1998). Kritische Erfolgsfaktoren von Post-Merger Integrationen. *M&A Review*, 2.

Picot, G. (Hrsg.) (2012a) Handbuch Mergers & Acquisitions: Planung – Durchführung – Integration (5. Auflage). Stuttgart: Schäffer-Poeschel Verlag.

Picot, G. (2012b). Personelle und kulturelle Integration. In G. Picot (Hrsg.), *Handbuch Mergers & Acquisitions: Planung – Durchführung – Integration* (5. Auflage). Stuttgart: Schäffer-Poeschel Verlag.

Raffel, F.-C. (2006). Familienunternehmen akquirieren Unternehmen anders. *M&A-Review*, 3.

Rigall, J., & Tarlatt, A. (2010). Strukturelle Integration als Herausforderung des Managements von Post Merger Integrationen. In G. Müller-Stewens, S. Kunisch, & A. Binder (Hrsg.), Mergers & acquisitions: Analysen, Trends und Best Practices. Stuttgart: Schäffer-Poeschel Verlag.

Rothenbücher, J., Niewiem, S., & Bovermann, J. (2012). Massgefertigt: M&A Synergien mit Augenmass. M&A-Review, 1.

Schäfer, M., & Blankenburg, D. (1997). Die Existenz und Mitwirkung des Firmeninhabers erleichtert den Zukaufsprozess.

Schreiner, A., Wirth, M., & Wirth, T. (2010). From Good to Great – Erfolgsfaktoren aus der Praxis in der Umsetzung aus Verkäuferperspektive. In G. Müller-Stewens, S. Kunisch, & A. Binder (Hrsg.), *Mergers and acquisitions: Analysen, Trends und Best Practices*. Stuttgart: Schäffer-Poeschel Verlag.

Spill, J. (2007). Warum jede zweite Transaktion scheitert. *M&A-Review*, 1.

Unger, M. (2007). *Handbuch Mergers & Acquisitions*. Wien: Linde.

Ungerath, M., & von Hoyningen-Huene, J. (2005). PMI: Integrationserfolg zwischen Konsens und Durchsetzungskraft. *M&A-Review*, 3.

Integration Management as a Gateway to Performance Transformation

2.1 Sustainable Integration Success Takes Longer than a Hundred Days

Top scores in a sports competition are the result of meticulous preparation. A bit of luck may play into it, however, a target-oriented preparatory phase is the be-all and end-all of success—and the basis for a sustainable performance improvement. The same holds true for integration management. What is important is the combination of "rapid" decisions and "slow" development work. In an integration project, key issues must be addressed head-on and rapidly, the right strings need to be pulled and decisions must be quick. After that, changes need to be given enough time to unfold and have their impact. A consistent performance improvement cannot be achieved without the determination to persistently optimize a company's organization. An integration process, on the other hand, is anything but routine, it is an exceptional phase. It is vital that the transition to everyday business operations and into everyday organizational procedures be not delayed. No one can integrate forever.

Meeting acquisition targets requires a sustainable and fine-tuned integration management.[1] But what does sustainable actually mean? In many cases, integration is not understood as a long-term process, but as something that has to be concluded the sooner the better. A series of practical examples indicate, however, that a company's integration is not a singular, project-related matter, but rather a regularly recurring process accompanied by learning effects.[2] Exploiting synergies by sharing know-how takes much longer than a hundred days. Integration is therefore no longer a clearly definable and temporally limited "project"; it is much rather an integral part of a corporate strategy.[3]

---

[1] Hackmann (2011, p. 221).
[2] Fuhrer (2007, p. 216 f).
[3] Gerds and Schewe (2014, p. 165 ff.) and Fuhrer (2007, p. 235).

The practical cases we have examined have revealed that successful high-performance organizations manage to trigger a mutual learning process in the course of integrations; they merge into a new corporate culture, commit to it, and eventually improve their combined performance—meaning that they reach a higher level of performance. We refer to this type of integration management as "performance transformation".[4] By means of a targeted change in staff attitude and behavior, the integration management increases a company's performance. Performance transformation is not limited to a specific project, but instead represents an ongoing process, a learning process within the framework of a respective corporate strategy.

We emphatically do not advocate that decisions concerning integration management be delayed or actively put off. Not by any means. Securing a company's pre-merger value, i.e. the company value before the merger and the existing core business, is of utmost importance. Such decisions are to be made rapidly for employees to know the integration targets and how this merger will affect each and every member of staff. Performance transformation as such, that is, the way to a higher level of performance, on the other hand, is considerably more time consuming.

Performance transformation can only take place on condition that the top priorities go beyond the merely financial synergies. Sprenger[5] claims that a company's main managerial goal must be that the shared management problem—in this case the integration challenge—is brought in line with customer benefit. The central question therefore has to be how customers can ultimately benefit from the completed acquisition. Companies must by all means observe customers and markets on a regular basis—in the sense of a continual organization and communication task.

At the same time, cultural aspects must be changed in a way that they foster a successful amalgamation of different organizations. Pivotal "soft" factors are the right attitude of staff, willingness to change, the determination to assume responsibility, the necessary stamina to implement these changes, and ultimately, the enthusiasm to reach a superior level in corporate development. Practice shows that 30% of all affected staff suffices to implement the desired changes.[6]

Despite these commendable intentions to put customers first and to give cultural change the necessary room to develop, these points in particular are often neglected.[7] Empirical studies reveal that the customer still does not take center stage in the integration process and cultural aspects are often taken into consideration too late. According to surveys, there is ample room for improvement in terms

---

[4]Schreiner et al. (2010, p. 302 ff).
[5]Sprenger (2012, p. 65, 166).
[6]Schreiner et al. (2010, p. 303 ff.).
[7]Deutsch and West (2010, p. 7).

2.1 Sustainable Integration Success Takes Longer than a Hundred Days

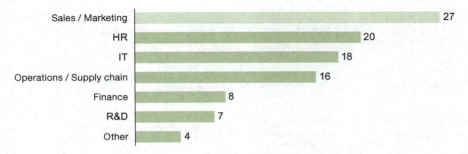

Fig. 2.1 In sales and marketing, HR and IT, there is ample room for improvement in terms of integration ability. Source: Deutsch and West (2010, p. 8)

of integration ability in sales and marketing departments, HR, but also IT (Fig. 2.1).[8]

Standardization of the acquisition and integration process as well as learning effects from comparable projects are essential conditions that will facilitate future integration projects. And this is exactly where high-performance organizations set the compasses.[9]

Performance transformation is applied to the most significant integration management problems; and resolving those produces a major leverage effect. Based on the neuralgic points that the previous chapter has elaborated on, we deduct the following five steps of successful performance transformation: the company DNA as the backbone of the integration office responsibility; the actual performance transformation as such; the exploitation of integration dynamics; target-oriented talent management; as well as integration monitoring (Figs. 2.2 and 2.3).

Expert View
by Dr. Philip Robinson, Stefan Rösch-Rütsche and Samy Walleyo (EY)
"It is never too early to initiate integration activities."

The spectrum of tasks of mergers and acquisitions (M&A) has drastically changed over recent years. While the 1990s and the beginning of this millennium saw a distinct emphasis on due diligence, as well as on the negotiations and the processing and closing of contracts, recent years have increasingly witnessed a need to regard an M&A transaction as an end-to-end process; a process that begins with strategy formation and ends when integration is completed. This widening of the spectrum of tasks naturally changes the roles of those who are in charge of mergers and acquisitions.

Most tasks concerning strategy formation and operative integration in the different business units are undoubtedly down to the executive management. Yet, consistent responsibility and control that comes from one hand only is a decisive factor for the success of a transaction. Both the strategy and its formation must be

---
[8] Deutsch and West (2010, p. 8).
[9] Fuhrer (2007, p. 214 f).

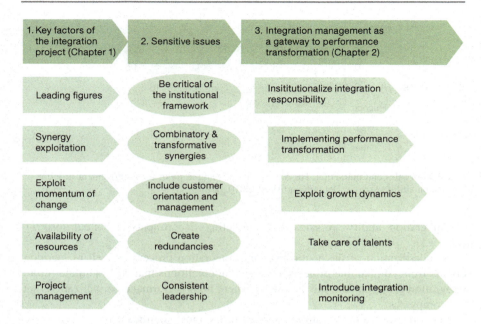

Fig. 2.2 In the course of integration, neuralgic points are transposed into a performance transformation concept. Source: Bergamin/Braun

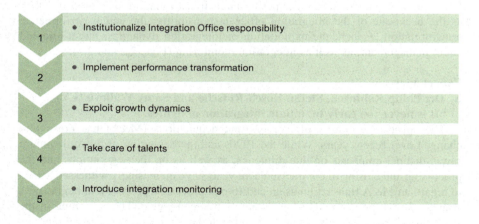

Fig. 2.3 Performance transformation concept. Source: Bergamin/Braun

fully understood and assumed to identify the right target companies, offer an appropriate price, and negotiate conclusive contracts on the basis of which integration can be planned and implemented.

In an acquisition, a consistent process is therefore of the essence. The protagonists in charge not only need to fully understand all the interdependencies with respect to content and temporal succession, but they also have to be aware of the fact that any decisions made before the signing will set the course for what follows after the closing of contract.

As consultants we have monitored such processes many times, and despite the variety of business segments and the company sizes, we have repeatedly observed the following fundamental points:

- It is never too early to initiate integration activities.
- Nothing outweighs the power of a vision and the credibility of a management.
- No two integrations are the same, and yet, respective experiences and employees with a wealth of integration experience are of great value.

Dr. Philip Robinson
Partner EY Switzerland
Stefan Rösch-Rütsche
Transaction Advisory Services Leader of EY Switzerland
Samy Walleyo
Operational Transactions Services of EY Germany, Austria and Switzerland

2.2 Institutionalize Integration Responsibility

Acquisitions often disappoint in the sense that they do not or only partly meet the expectations that have been placed in them. They are not successful, as they fail to fully exploit the potential that comes with a merger or acquisition. We believe that one of the main reasons for this disappointing result is that the responsibilities for the exploitation of the integration potential and synergies within an organization are not clearly assigned (Fig. 2.4).

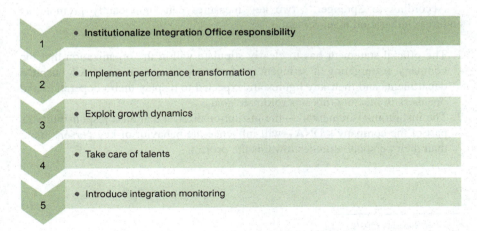

Fig. 2.4 Performance transformation concept—step 1. Source: Bergamin/Braun

As discussed earlier, small and mid-caps distinguish themselves by their lean structures. This—in itself a positive fact—means that their management's temporal and often also operative commitment is rather demanding. For a management to work well under such circumstances, the following imperatively implies: clear organizational structures, with a focus on critical issues, and a stringent course of action that focuses on implementation. These tall orders may sometimes exceed the capabilities of the best of management teams, notably so when there are simply too many projects running at the same time that are treated with great urgency, or when certain business segments turn into problem cases and the management directs most of its attention to them.

The practical cases that we have examined demonstrate that small and mid-caps are particularly challenged, due to the dominance of their leadership personalities and the work overload as a result of an accumulation of mandates. A select few key figures set the pace and all business decisions revolve around them. As a consequence, the focus on the integration process is often lost and improvement potentials lie dormant. In the worst case, these unsuccessful integration attempts will detrimentally affect a company's survival.

In such situations, large companies and corporations fall back on a so-called project organization or governance structure that usually consists of four parts: the steering committee, the integration office, the implementation team, and the core process team.[10] This kind of arrangement, however, often exceeds the possibilities of small and mid-caps.

Our recommendation is to make integration responsibility a part of the company DNA. This governance integration office entails an institutional responsibility with the aim of an enduring, long-term and sustainable integration of acquired companies. Widely accepted on an institutional and personal level, the person in charge—i.e. the integration manager—should be able to scrutinize company decisions and be willing to assume the role of advocatus diaboli (devil's advocate) with certain issues concerning the integration management.

According to Sprenger,[11] two key measures can significantly promote an enduring integration management.

1. The official statement has to clearly stipulate within the organization that the company is targeting a stringent performance transformation. All business departments and their key figures are expected to display their cooperation and openness in meeting this superordinate goal.
2. The institutional framework—the institutionalized integration responsibility as part of the company's DNA—will influence the behavior of key persons more than their personal attitudes towards the project.

---

[10]Müller-Stewens (2010, p. 12).
[11]Sprenger (2012, p. 88, also see p. 49).

2.2 Institutionalize Integration Responsibility

Sprenger therefore concludes—and so do we—that the determination of individual leadership figures is not enough to change a particular mode of conduct. The crucial element is its anchoring, i.e. its being an integral part of the company DNA.

Creating such an appropriate and separate position in the company management simply exceeds the possibilities of many small and mid-caps. It need not adamantly be a new position; a manager may assume the responsibility for a persistent integration management alongside other tasks. What is crucial, however, is that this person is given enough time to complete this task. Institutional anchoring emerges as a clearly defined responsibility and objective. It is given to an integration management leader. At the same time, this person's performance becomes measurable.

Should key persons with responsibilities in the integration process assume another full-time responsibility, they benefit from their awareness that once the project concludes, they will be able to return to their former roles in the management organization and therefore shed the extra work load. This was the case with the acquisitions of Gate Gourmet: the integration manager was also the head of purchasing department. Upon conclusion of the mega acquisition of SAS Service Partner, his work load as integration manager dropped, which gave him ample time again to focus on his role as head of purchasing department.

Depending on the situation, this integration responsibility can be limited to a specific project, i.e. be of a temporary nature. In the case of mega acquisitions, this may make perfect sense. Independently of the sphere of action of the integration office, the progress of the integration management has to be the subject of discussion on a corporate level; for instance twice a year, in the management or board of directors on occasion of the launch of the business plan in spring, and the subsequent planning meeting in autumn. This ensures that integration has its place on the managerial agenda and is paid attention to on a regular basis.

When it comes to the definition of the roles of those responsible for the integration office, we have to differentiate between a supporting function in the integration process and the actual responsibility for successful integration as such—the integration leader. These two functions may be assigned to different people or a single person. The supporting function may include the following scope of duties[12]:

- Leading and monitoring of the ongoing integration process,
- Setting up a control system to monitor integration status (e.g. to exploit synergy targets) that will then be communicated to the management in charge and the board of directors,
- Supporting the management in connection with all questions concerning integration management,
- Assuming a coordinating function in integration questions with respect to finance, business departments, human resources, communication, etc.,
- Devising a decision and escalation process,

---

[12]Habeck et al. (2013, p. 65 ff.), Hackmann (2011, p. 174) and McLetchie (2010, p. 31 f).

- And data collection and document management (particularly of new knowledge).

The ultimate responsibility for integration success lies with the management that has proposed the acquisition and represents the acquisition in front of the company committees. The person in charge of integration cannot delegate this task to an executive department. Both management and board of directors should rightfully insist on hearing reports about the state of the project straight from the horse's mouth as it were.

The responsibility for the integration office distinguishes itself by its cross-departmental function. Its measures are put in place cross-functionally within and between various business units and divisions. Their particular organizational positioning can accelerate integration measures and enhance their target-orientation to beat measures in an ordinary organization to it.

To conclude we see two possible forms of organization. In option one (see Fig. 2.5), the person in charge of the operative management assumes both the role of integration leader and is in charge of the integration office at the same time. This person reports to the steering committee. In option two, the person in charge of integration introduces the integration office as an executive department and with it its responsibility. The person who this role is assigned to assumes all supporting functions within the framework of integration in a bid to reduce the integration leader's work load. The integration leader, on the other hand, accounts for the project opposite the steering committee and ensures a constant, end-to-end flow of information.

An interview with Dr. Renato Fassbind, member of the board of directors at SwissRe, on the topic of integration manager:

"The responsibility for the merger lies with the operative management."

Mr. Fassbind, what are the reasons why half of all acquisitions are unsuccessful?

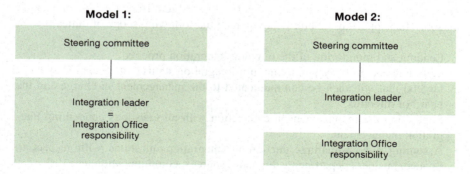

Fig. 2.5 Organizing the chief integration office. Source: Bergamin/Braun

2.2 Institutionalize Integration Responsibility

Many acquisitions are unsuccessful, because albeit the management releases a bold statement, it is often a case of all bark and no action. If acquisition projects are run by a strategy responsible who is largely unaffected by operative processes, there is a distinct risk that this out of touch approach during the integration phase will backfire. An integration project has to be planned meticulously and the defined milestones are to be implemented stringently. Measuring the target achievements during the project phase is on a manager's agenda as much as the critical follow-up variance analysis of an integration project.

What is important in the run-up to an integration project?

The responsibility for an acquisition project emphatically lies with the operative management. Thus, the operative management must be included in the decision and evaluation processes from the start. Targets, milestones, synergies etc. need to be outlined. It is in the hands of the operative management to decide what goals are going to be reached by integration, and synergies also have to be identified. Only then can the management be made accountable at a later stage.

Integration and significant processes of change often go hand in hand. Are there forms of integration that are particularly promising?

The way to successful integration is greatly individual and depends on the specific situation of a particular project or deal. I have seen successful integrations that are the result of seismic shifts. On the other hand, I have witnessed integration projects where the autonomy of the acquired company was largely preserved—and successfully so. Change management and synergy exploitation per se are not always the best option. The best possible method as a rule depends on the case in question. No two deals can be integrated the same way.

What significance do you attribute to HR policy in an integration project?

Involving the right people in strategically critical projects is pivotal. An integration project is an ideal platform for talents to demonstrate their abilities. This phase can also be a golden opportunity to part with weak and unsuitable key persons.

In your view, what does optimum project organization in integration management look like?

In choosing those responsible for integration, the top management has to investigate whether they have the necessary skills and knowledge to cope with the duress of integration, whether they have enough time and whether they display the required level of commitment. As mentioned before, leadership persons have to completely merge with the project, as they are critical to its success. It may make sense to appoint someone to work closely with the head of integration, a sort of right hand; someone who would be in charge of the integration office until the end of the project. This would create sufficient resources for professional implementation of the project.

Does an integration office on a project level suffice to guarantee overall integration success?

Stringent integration reporting is a must alongside integration management on a project level. This way, both target achievement and status report can be processed in a transparent manner and be forwarded to company management and board of directors. The CFO is typically in charge of processing this kind of information; its

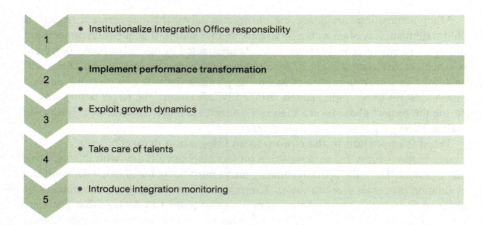

Fig. 2.6 Performance transformation concept—step 2. Source: Bergamin/Braun

communication to the outside world on the other hand rests with the operative manager.

2.3 Implementing Performance Transformation

2.3.1 Four Dimensions

To achieve a lasting performance transformation (Fig. 2.6), the integration potential that comes with the acquired companies must be exploited to its fullest. The aim is to strengthen its success potential in accordance with the project strategy. The following important levers add value in the course of integration[13]:

- Securing the company's pre-merger value and its core business,
- Exploiting synergy potential in order to increase efficiency,
- Searching for transformational synergies that trigger a radical change in functions, processes or business segments.

The guidelines for these integration efforts have to be established. There is no universal recipe when it comes to integration management; the specific context of acquisitions essentially determines the requirements to the integration management and defines the scope of the different options.[14] Guidelines are derived from the company strategy and determine how intensely and comprehensively these integration efforts have to be conducted and what focal points are going to be established.

---

[13]Deutsch and West (2010, p. 6).
[14]Müller-Stewens, (2010, p. 5).

2.3 Implementing Performance Transformation

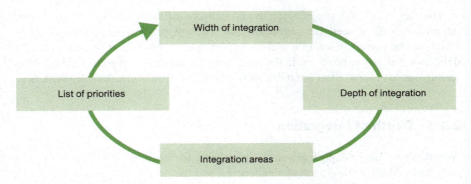

Fig. 2.7 Individual performance transformation design. Source: Jansen and Brügger (2012, p. 665); see also: Schreiner et al. (2010, p. 302ff)

Integration management therefore becomes a critical tool for implementing company strategy.

We distinguish four dimensions of categorization (Fig. 2.7):

- **Depth of integration**: Does the integration management intend to narrow its focus on the traditional business or instead widen it beyond its current business segment?
- **Width of integration**: How radical should the process of change be in the course of integration?
- **Areas of integration**: What aspects should be of prime concern in the course of integration?
- **List of priorities**: How strongly will integration efforts be influenced and what is their aim?

2.3.2 Width of Integration

In terms of content, integration designs may point into different directions. On one hand, a decision has to be made as to whether integration targets a widening of the core business or opening up of new business segments. On the other hand, growth intentions or the need for restructuring have to be taken into consideration as well. The focus of integration therefore depends on the option that is chosen.

An organization above all needs to decide whether it wants to continue to focus on its traditional core business or whether it is open to exploring new business segments. Concentrating on its core business means that optimizations and further developments should be given priority. Should the company opt to explore new business segments, it must be open to expanding the performance portfolio beyond its current state.

Then again, growth projects require an entirely different managerial style than integration with a need for restructuration. Growth projects need a razor-sharp vision of the company's future and its impact, and it means that in many cases a deliberate risk has to be taken. In the case of restructuration, companies tend to take an introspective look. Staff are more worried, often there is considerable resistance.

2.3.3 Depth of Integration

According to Haspeslagh/Jemison,[15] the criteria for depth of integration are, for one, the need for strategic interdependencies, and the desire for organizational and cultural autonomy, for another. From there, four categories of integration depth can be deducted: turnaround, stabilization, symbiosis, and absorption (Fig. 2.8).

The types of integration strategy referred to as "turnaround" and "stabilization" are typically the preferred methods for financial investors such as private equity funds. The degree of integration is the lowest, and changes within an organization do not automatically lead to changes in its partner organization. The complexity of the integration process is therefore straightforward and manageable. The integration type referred to as "stabilization" is often seen in connection with acquisitions that aim to diversify.

The types referred to as "symbiosis" (partial integration) and "absorption" (full integration) distinguish themselves by their exploitation of strategic interdependencies. These types mostly apply to strategic investors. With symbiosis in particular, expansion intentions are in the foreground. Both types of integration aim to exploit synergies, which increases the complexity of the integration process.

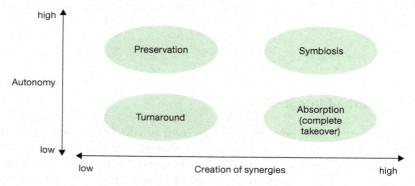

Fig. 2.8 Types of integration and rising demands on post-merger managements. Source: Jansen and Brügger (2012, p. 677); also see: Müller-Stewens, Konzeptionelle Entscheidungen (2010, p. 9), also see: Bucerius (2004, p. 14 ff.), also see: Hackmann (2011, p. 177 ff)

---

[15]Haspeslagh and Jemison (1992).

2.3 Implementing Performance Transformation

In the case of symbiosis, a company is acquired, it undergoes a process of change but keeps a certain degree of autonomy. It is not fully absorbed or integrated. The parent company displays clear signs of willingness to co-evolve, in other words, it wants to change.[16] Absorption denotes the highest degree of integration.

The company strategy determines which one of the four integration types it will conduct. A company's choice of strategy therefore always reflects the degree of autonomy of the acquired units and how much weight will be given to integration efforts. The integration crash barriers can be deducted from this choice.

2.3.4 Areas of Integration

A next step addresses the question of which areas should be integrated. Synergy exploitation is essentially possible along the following areas of integration: strategy, organization, business segments, HR and culture, range of products and supplier structure, systems and processes such as taxes and legislation (Fig. 2.9).

High-performance enterprises fundamentally differentiate between two types of synergies: combinational and transformational. They strive to develop into both directions.[17] Achieving combinational synergies is on the agenda of many companies. These synergies are typically achieved by economies of scale or cross-selling of existing products. In most cases they are risk-free, and are easily quantifiable. In the course of due diligence during the transaction process, they often take center stage. Truly successful companies, however, also manage to generate and use transformative synergies. The merger specifically serves to

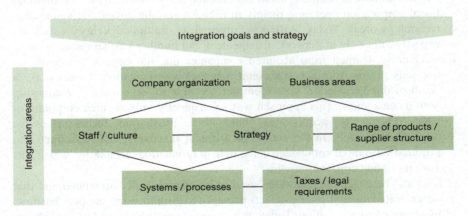

Fig. 2.9 Areas of integration. Source: Unger (2007, p. 878)

---

[16]Müller-Stewens (2006, p. 9).
[17]McLetchie and West (2010, p. 12).

scrutinize traditions and habits and to break new ground starting from the comfort of an existing platform. This kind of synergy creation is more prone to risks, complex and often goes hand in hand with feelings of insecurity.

These synergy types are only applied to selected areas of integration. The following gives a few examples of combinational synergies:

Integration ensues along the strategic positioning of the newly merged companies.[18] The focus lies on a targeted use and expansion of existing skills.

Eliminating duplication and the streamlining of organizations are typical examples of combinational synergies. Standardization of systems and processes are of utmost importance, especially with volume-driven companies. It increases business processes, which has a positive cost effect.

Capitalization on tax advantages can be a key driver for the integration management. Tax advantages may be an important trigger for a takeover, and they play a non-negligible role in the subsequent business performance.

The following examples of transformational synergies illustrate that they are more complicated to implement than combinational synergies:

In 2010, ABB acquired the American company Ventyx, a key player in energy management software and smart grids. Having said that, ABB itself is a leader in power systems, but Ventyx brought a wealth of expertise and network management to the organization and all the IT and communication technologies in connection with it. Thanks to this merger, ABB moved from producing AC and DC motors, generators, steam turbines and transformers to integral multinational corporation operating mainly in robotics and the power and automation technology areas. Today, ABB has purposefully multiplied Ventyx's software expertise, not only in network management, but in other business units as well.

Gate Gourmet learned from acquired companies that the customer care of key accounts profits from a key account manager who is stationed locally. As a result of this knowledge, Gate Gourmet was able to forge a close relationship with its customers. This approach was subsequently implemented corporation-wide. Thanks to acquisitions, innovative distribution techniques were established as well. In the course of different takeovers, Gate Gourmet also acquired substantial knowledge in the field of production technology, which was also multiplied corporation-wide.

A food and beverage company that used to be commercially orientated and that concentrated on high-price products managed to push forward into bulk business by means of an acquisition. Today, this company provides large fast food chains all over the world with its products. Without this acquisition, the company is more than likely to have remained in its niche.

One of the largest ground and cargo handling services corporations in the world managed to grow exponentially through its multi acquisitions. When it reached a

---

[18] See Hackmann (2011, p. 224).

critical size, the foundation of an equipment rental and leasing company seemed like a good idea. The company was intended to manage the entire fleet of vehicles and all the machinery of the ground and cargo handling services corporation with the aim to lease it to the parent company and external clients alike. And there it was, the birth of an intriguing, new business idea.

2.3.5 List of Priorities

The array for possible integration measures is vast, and the risk for companies to spread themselves too thinly is high. Companies thus do well to compile an individual list of priorities for their integration efforts. We thereby differentiate three dimensions: "critical to success", "urgent" und "extensive". The sub-systems that are be integrated—i.e. business segments, functional areas, regions, branches or subsidiaries, plants or factories, etc.—are to be lined up according to these dimensions. For example, if buyer and target organization operate on different IT systems, the question has to be how critical to success, urgent, or extensive the transition to a unified IT system would be.

Beyond the degree of urgency and significance, this list further indicates along what rules the collaboration between the acquiring and the target company can be established. The general atmosphere during the integration process is decisive. A climate of mutual understanding, readiness to cooperate as well as the resources that can be allocated are important parameters for a constructive cooperation (Fig. 2.10).[19]

A democratic course of action is based on an intense feedback culture. Integration projects provide learning effects for both buyer and the acquired company. Time provided, this procedure is highly recommendable. Two fundamental questions have to be asked:

- What can the acquiring company learn from the target organization?
- Is there anything within the new framework that has attracted the target company's attention?[20]

If integration topics are critical to success, urgent and ensue extensive or steep cuts to the organization, the democratic course of action described above may be unrewarding. Receptiveness to impulses and readiness to accept feedback is key, even in this situation. What has emerged, however, is that extensive measures of change require a word of command and cannot be found in a democratic consensus.

---

[19]Fuhrer (2007, p. 223).
[20]Also see Fuhrer (2007, p. 221 ff).

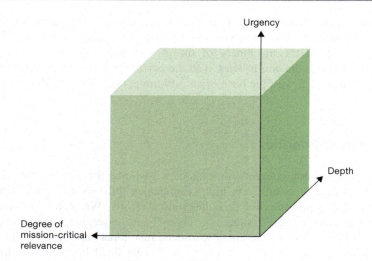

Fig. 2.10 Prioritization of integration measures. Source: Bergamin/Braun. See also: Müller-Stewens et al. (2010, p. 10)

2.3.6 Individual Design of Performance Transformation

Individual performance transformation as a form of integration emerges from the specific design of the four integration dimensions. The following will elaborate on the two different forms of "diversification" and "focus" by way of example.

Type "diversification": distinguishes itself by its diversifying tendency (great width of integration). The autonomy of symbiosis remains untouched, but at the same time—wherever it applies—this autonomy is integrated and therefore altered (depth of integration). In the example of the ground handling services corporation, the aim was to multiply and extend its core competences (areas of integration). In the sense of a democratic course of action, both buyer and acquired company were expected to learn from the other's wealth of experience (list of priorities).

Type "focus": concentrates on its traditional core business (narrow width of integration). Integration is to be achieved in the form of absorption (great depth of integration), and existing processes and systems are to be exploited even better through acquisitions (areas of integration). Due to its great urgency, the buyer sets the pace (list of priorities).

Practical example of width of integration and depth of integration in an international context: acquisition of DocMorris (Germany) and Zur Rose Group (Switzerland/Austria).
Zur Rose Group delivers medicines to the right place, at the right time so to speak. The Group in this sense acts as a mail-order chemist or pharmacy and as wholesaler of medical products to doctors in Switzerland, Austria and Germany. Its firm

2.3 Implementing Performance Transformation

position with doctors and pharmacists warrants for its medical and pharmaceutical know-how, Swiss quality and reliability.

Zur Rose saw a distinct growth opportunity by acquiring DocMorris in 2012. The Group's turnover almost doubled to CHF 1 billion, in no time. The share of turnover in Germany and Austria before the acquisition was at about 10%; after the takeover, half of the Group's turnover was generated by Germany.

This is an example of an acquisition that targeted a diversification in terms of distribution channels and geographical presence. Concerning the depth of integration, a symbiotic approach was followed. Sales remained autonomous, but value-adding organizational processes up front—i.e. from purchasing to stock-holding, as well as supporting functions—were streamlined wherever possible.

DocMorris is a mail-order pharmacy from where patients can order their prescription and over the counter medicaments on the internet, or offline from a catalogue. Zur Rose Switzerland possesses a wealth of specialist knowledge and experience as a wholesaler to doctors. The company delivers medicaments to physicians, care and retirement homes and other health service providers.

The synergies that the merger created in this commercial enterprise emerged from the following areas:

- Increased purchasing power and a better negotiating position when purchasing from drug manufacturers,
- Standardization of IT systems and synergies in logistic operation and warehouse capacity,
- A standardized financial reporting system.

The key persons in the sales, logistics and financial departments therefore were closely involved in the integration project. The goals were a bundled market presence for the purchasing department and standardized operative processes in sales and distribution and reporting.

For the company's image to the outside world, the two brand names "Zur Rose" and "DocMorris" were consciously maintained, the former being the physician, the latter the patient brand.

After the merger, sales and customer approach remain decentralized and in the hands of each national organization. Tight regulation and stringent quality monitoring are important characteristics of the pharmaceutical industry, which is one of the reasons why the Group decided to delegate sales and distribution to each national organization. Standardization in sales took no priority.

Walter Oberhänsli, delegate of the board of directors and CEO Zur Rose Group, attributes the reason for this successful integration to the chemistry between the managers in charge as well as the trust that they are able to share.

- Personal relationships on a management and business segment level were emphasized from the start. Regular visits on site always began with some sort of evening entertainment and a social event. Eight hours of the following day were dedicated to discussing all imminent projects in detail. Considerable time

and effort were invested into this cooperation, it therefore goes far beyond a superficial collaboration. Oberhänsli likes to refer to it as coaching, which he wants to promote on all corporative levels.
- Integration is understood as collaboration and interaction in one. Depending on the respective strengths that the buying company or the target organization bring to the table. DocMorris was already running an SAP business software before the acquisition. When it came to finding a corporation-wide solution, it was not AXAPTA—the system that Zur Rose had actually envisaged as a viable option—but the target organization's existing SAP system that was chosen.
- Oberhänsli visited DocMorris just a few days after the takeover. The company's former owner, on the other hand, was never on site. On his first visit, Oberhänsli already noticed the crammed working conditions. He literally saw some room for improvement, and no sooner said than done, the company moved into a new office building. Oberhänsli's systematic approach left a very positive impression with all DocMorris staff and was spectacularly motivating.

By acquiring DocMorris, Zur Rose straightforward targeted transformative synergies. DocMorris paves the way for the corporation towards digitization. The acquisition of a key player such as DocMorris has the potential to define new industry standards: the two most important levers for this are the introduction of electronic prescriptions and the rejection of rigid price regulation. If these two crucial parameters are altered, attractive development potentialities for the corporation will arise in Germany.

Logistics automatization is the second leverage point for transformative synergies. Manuel processes should largely be taken over by automated systems.

Oberhänsli looks ahead and does not want to dwell on past mistakes; having said that, the following are his lessons learnt:

- An acquiring organization's claim to set the pace and on its terms only, will not pay off. In most cases, such a stringent approach simply demotivates the company's management.
- In an acquisition, financial management tools are particularly critical; if they do not function and if leading indicators for the measurement of business management lack, they may have a negative effect.

The Zur Rose Group example demonstrates how the aspect of internationality is to be taken into account in addition to earlier mentioned dimensions of synergy exploitation in transnational transactions. This generic example illustrates that alongside all efforts in terms of comprehensive synergy exploitation and corporation-wide standardization, the peculiarities of the local organizations in the respective countries must be taken into account. These local claims may even have more of a stake than the demand for comprehensive standardization.

2.3 Implementing Performance Transformation

Expert View
Only if an M&A transaction exploits its potential with respect to value drivers and boosts its market position, will customers, employees and investors be able to thoroughly understand the purpose of an M&A transaction and ultimately embrace it.

by Hans Hess, President of Swissmem (Swiss Association of Mechanical and Electrical Engineering Industries)

Companies implement their global strategies driven by impulses from within, but increasingly employ external impulses from mergers and acquisitions. For a multitude of reasons. Good M&A strategies, in fact, are essentially part of an overall strategy that increases both growth and value. Many companies proceed this way in a bid to gain time in their efforts to meet their strategic targets. Such growth efforts almost inevitably ensue certain risks and therefore require a professional management process in order to be successful. The post-merger integration phase (PMI) in particular is attributed a key role during the implementation of mergers and acquisitions. Regrettably, this phase is still often underrated. The search for suitable target companies, due diligence and the closing of contract often only represent as little as a third of the entire task at hand. The remaining two thirds of the challenge begin once a transaction has been completed. As a result, executive managements that tackle the PMI phase comprehensively and rigorously—preferably even before the transaction is completed—will ultimately find this course of action rewarding. The fate of PMI is often sealed straight after the closing; the crucial moment when unwavering commitment to the cause begins. Project management and project controlling are key elements of the PMI phase. The mere merging of the organizations and leadership teams involved, however, is not the main issue, and nor are other PMI "duties" such as consolidating accounting and reporting systems. The focus must be on bringing people together from different companies with different company cultures. This company culture in fact will be substantially changed in the wake of a merger, and in the case of a successful merger, very often an entirely new integrated company culture is created. Employees of the acquired company will be feeling apprehensive during this time; soft skills are decisive in this case, along with excellent communication skills and perseverance of the management of the buying company. Integration communication is essential, but so is the formation of a PMI task force and a comprehensive integration road map. The main goal is to fully exploit the strengths of both companies in order to achieve the desired synergy effects. In many cases, the focus still predominantly lies on achieving cost synergies. The actual and sustainable benefit of an M&A transaction, however, will only manifest itself, if potentials with respect to value drivers and a boost in market position of the new common company are exploited to their most. Only this way will customers, employees and investors be able to thoroughly understand the purpose of an M&A transaction and ultimately embrace it.

Hans Hess, President of Swissmem (Association MEM Industries)
Chairman and member of the board of various Swiss industrial enterprises

2.3.7 Checklist 1: Scaling and Standardization in an International Context

The following chart indicates the different subject areas and suggests appropriate procedures.

Scaling and standardization	Yes	No limited	Critical aspects	Suggestions
HR: remuneration and incentive system		X	Possible differences in national wage and purchasing power; an integrated and internationally competitive benefit scheme for the executive management is key during post-merger phases	If in doubt, retain local remuneration systems. The incentive logic must remain unchanged
HR: training concepts		X	Different demands on training, depending on the level of seniority in the organization and the demands of international collaborations	Standardization in as much as there is a local benefit
HR: exchange	X		Wage differentials are prone to discord	Set clear guidelines regarding an international exchange
Other HR processes		X	Company DNAs need not be merged at any cost	Adaptation of structures, function diagrams, boards and values
IT: acquisition of hardware and software		X	Purchasing locally (e.g. licenses) may be cheaper than centralized purchases	Exploit bundling advantages by respecting local idiosyncrasies
Finances: reporting format	X		Standardization is feasible and makes sense	Clear guidelines and implementation monitoring
Finances: reporting systems	X		Standardization is feasible and makes sense	Clear guidelines and implementation monitoring
Leadership and control guidelines	X		Standardization is feasible and makes sense	Clear guidelines and implementation monitoring
Research and development		X	Talents may not be internationally mobile; research environment and possibilities outside the company are also decisive with respect to choice of location	Highly critical HR topic; secure talents' loyalty to the company and keep them motivated

(continued)

Purchasing	X		Bundling of purchasing power	Rapid synergy achievements are possible. This area requires flawless and multiple-integrated information systems. In practice, in an integrated purchasing organization there are thought and operation barriers to overcome
Production	X		Labor and procurement costs, currency risk	In an increasingly globalized world economy, many manufacturing companies have a track record of outsourcing parts of production to low cost countries
Marketing: branding		X	Check for local peculiarities	Maximum standardization whilst taking local restrictions into account
Marketing: customer relation management		X	The significance of standardization depends on the business segment	Maximum standardization whilst taking local restrictions into account
Sales		X	A local customer approach is important in many business segments	In order for customers not to lose interest, they must be center stage, particularly in the phase straight after the acquisition. For this reason, the sales department should not be turned upside down in a first merger step
Logistics	X		Critical mass and standardized procedures in many cases make up for the higher costs of transport in the case of a transnational centralization of a company's sales and distribution	Synergies of logistics must be aligned with purchasing, production and sales

2.4 Exploit Growth Dynamics

To conclude, every merger or acquisition has a sustainable influence on the companies involved, and it triggers diverse processes of change. The course of action in the actual integration project decides whether (a) efforts focus more on optimizing existing internal structures, or (b) acquisition politics trigger an outward growth dynamic (Fig. 2.11).

Fig. 2.11 Performance transformation concept—step 3. Source: Bergamin/Braun

Empirical studies[21] reveal that market and customer-related factors have a substantial influence on the success of a merger. The mere concentration on cost synergies and alignment of internal activities, structures, processes and systems, however, is no guarantee for positive effects of the same scale.

According to Sprenger,[22] a management's main task is to align leadership problems with customer benefit (see also Sect. 1). How can customers profit from a recent acquisition? A close look at the customers and markets will provide the answer; this customer and market awareness in turn must be understood as an unyielding organization and communication task.

Informing customers and staff is indispensable in creating a positive atmosphere that will promote growth. Such an approach seizes the growth momentum in the wake of an acquisition and strives to maintain it. Companies are advised to promote feelings of confidence and assurance concerning the merger in a bid for the sales department to rapidly gain new customers. Success messages evidently boost people's confidence to critically examine existing portfolios and adapt them accordingly.[23]

Customer and market communication has to be immediate and nip potential insecurities during the integration process in the bud. Anything that may make a customer abandon ship should be avoided. With a change of ownership in particular, customers need to be reassured of their benefit and the company has to bear witness to its resolve to continue to deliver, in order to increase customer retention. In the course of a growth strategy, tangible improvements may result alongside purely emotional aspects. One goal might perhaps be to streamline the product and service programs of two companies. Cross-selling and bundling can fundamentally improve performance promise and customer orientation.

---

[21]Bucerius (2004, p. 16).

[22]Sprenger (2012, p. 65, 166).

[23]Deutsch and West (2010, p. 8) and Gupta et al. (2010, p. 37 ff).

2.4 Exploit Growth Dynamics

The acquisition of SAS Service Partner demonstrates the boost that the overall Gate Gourmet organization received thanks to savvy integration management. It triggered further acquisitions that opened up new markets and a range of new products.

> **Practical Example**
> The acquisition of SAS Service Partner by Gate Gourmet was a trigger factor for the quantum leap of Gate Gourmet to global airline caterer.
> **"Buying is easy."** (Wolfgang Werlé, former president of the board of directors of Gate Gourmet Group)
> Gategroup (formerly Gate Gourmet Group) is the leading independent global provider of products, services and solutions related to a passenger's onboard experience. In 128 kitchens in 32 countries, Gategroup prepares more than 500,000 meals a day.
> Gate Gourmet Group was founded as Gate Group Management AG, its roots are in the former Swissair catering activities. Wolfgang Werlé was president of the board of directors and CEO, formally in charge of business development with LSG Sky Chefs Catering, a subsidiary of German Lufthansa.
> In August 1994, Gate Gourmet acquired the catering business (airlines and trains) of Swedish SAS Service Partner (SSP) with a revenue of CHF 500 million and 32 locations in 13 countries. The CHF 250 million acquisition doubled Gate Gourmet's revenues and made the company the worldwide third largest caterer with 13,000 staff in 64 locations in 21 countries, and an annual aggregate turnover of around CHF 1 billion.
> The integration of SAS Service Partner proved a complete success and triggered a growth dynamic that led to a quantum leap in the following years. One of the reasons for this success was that the team under the leadership of Wolfgang Werlé managed to skillfully deploy the growth dynamic that had been initiated by the SAS acquisition and transfuse it one to one to Gate Gourmet. It transformed Gate Gourmet into a global catering company.
> According to Werlé, the main challenge was that David had taken on Goliath and not vice versa. SAS had originally planned to team up with the American Dobbs company, not with little Gate Gourmet in Switzerland. SAS was hoping for more autonomy through a merger with Dobbs. The idea was that Dobbs would continue to serve the US market—SAS would continue to focus on the European market. But when two European competitors merge, the integration process reaches a new level of complexity.

With the benefit of hindsight, Werlé's conclusions are as follows:

- Rapid decisions are crucial. The new top management—comprising the chief executive, CFO and the HR responsible—was appointed straight away.

- The integration team was equally represented by members of Gate Gourmet and SAS Service Partner, in an effort to reflect the idea of partnership.
  - In a deliberate decision for temporally limited double staffing, a representative of Gate Gourmet and SAS Service Partner each was assigned to key positions in marketing, sales and purchasing, production and integration office.
  - The new team consisted of highly motivated, up-to-date people with a profound knowledge and an impressive track record, as well as opinion leaders from both companies.
  - Six months into the project saw the fine-tuning and the transition to the ordinary organization; double staffing was replaced by permanent solutions.
- A ground-breaking kick-off meeting was held in Montreux, where all the executives met for the first time. The chair of the board of directors of Gate Gourmet and Swissair Group made ardent speeches that soon managed to convince even the hard-core doubters of the great benefits of integration. Work meetings took place the same day, people got to know each other and it was not before long that a spirit of optimism took over.
- An external HR consultant was hired to conduct management assessments in both organizations. It quickly became evident where the important talents were. Those who were not in prominent roles already, were "parked", on stand-by for assignments to come.
- Werlé held monthly so-called town hall meetings (information meetings) in which the executive management exchanged views on goals and milestones, the project's current state, success messages and problem issues. Werlé visited every location, sought out all the frontline employees and those in the business units, and thereby quickly developed a feel for the general atmosphere and the state of the integration process. Wherever he went, he always brought Swiss chocolate with him, a strong symbol for his understanding of the company and the newly gained shared identity.
- Werlé attaches utmost importance to employee contact. He thought it vital to include staff right from the start and so create ideal starting conditions. For this matter, the HR responsible was attributed a key role. From day one, all key personnel knew what their new contracts in Switzerland would entail with respect to their salaries, relocation modalities, down to their children's schools. For those who decided to return to Scandinavia for the weekend, HR organized low-fare airline tickets and greatly facilitated all transfer modalities.
- Staff loyalty was pivotal for Werlé, but so was customer retention. Customers too were regularly kept in the loop about the integration process. And soon enough, customers too began to see the benefit of this acquisition; they were able to enjoy even more professional processes, and they benefited from an even greater geographical presence of Gate Gourmet.
- In the catering industry, great significance is attached to production. Unsurprisingly, Werlé thought it vital to ensure that production processes could continue unhindered by integration.

2.5 Take Care of Talents

In small and mid-caps, the executive manager and the chief financial officer usually carry the principal responsibility for the integration success. Even if they have to answer for either success or failure, they are often constrained to delegate integration efforts to other persons in the organization (Fig. 2.12).

For this reason, the question of resources is a perfectly valuable one. Resources must be planned and allocated in advance, and their costs must flow into the assessment of the company before integration actually commences. That said, it is advisable that companies can always resort to enough talents to assign to new tasks. With a lack of resources, the company is not prepared for sudden and urgent problems or vital strategic projects. Sprenger[24] for instance thus demands a certain degree of duplication in the leadership team, so called adaptation reserves, in order for the executive management to better handle unplanned events such as acquisition projects.[25] Talent management creates a pool of leadership persons who will be available for future key projects. On the buyer's side, the right talents must be identified, developed and retained. The target company's main goal must be to quickly assess the quality of the management in place and possible gaps, so that the leadership team can be composed in accordance with what is required.

> An interview with Dr. Philippe Hertig, partner Egon Zehnder International, on the subject of assessing executive management and talents:

"Transparency generates security and motivation."

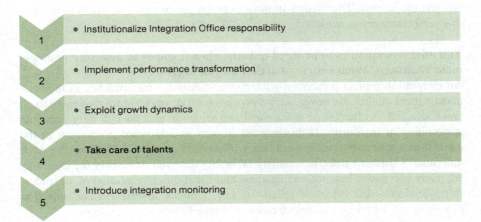

Fig. 2.12 Performance transformation concept—step 4. Source: Bergamin/Braun

---

[24]Sprenger (2012, p. 219 f).
[25]DePamphilis (2003, p. 318).

Mr. Hertig, it is beyond question that the quality of the management is one of the key success factors in integration management. What is the right moment during the integration process to tackle this topic?
We often notice that decision makers are mostly concerned with due diligence of financial, legal and technical aspects during the assessment phase. In my opinion, however, due diligence of staff is important in equal measure. Having said that, the prospects of success of an acquisition adamantly depends on the quality of the management. This assessment regrettably often does not take place in the run up to a project. Admittedly, legislation issues might be a reason to delay this assessment, mostly due to non-compete covenants. Yet, a suitable alternative could be an external assessment of the management to get a first impression of the managerial skills in place. For all intents and purposes, an objective and comprehensive assessment of executive staff has to be conducted as quickly as possible to safeguard the success to integration.

From an HR point of view, what are the key aspects of the integration phase?
Very often the management's primary concern is how to label the newly created organizational entities. I believe that the more pressing issue is to establish both strategy and company culture and then align the perfect leadership strategy with it. A strategy workshop would be suitable to contemplate these issues. Once the nature of strategy implementation and company culture has been established, all leadership behavior and the necessary skills for key people may be deducted from there. Typically, only a handful of leadership skills, and therefore leadership behavior, are ultimately decisive for the assessment and selection process. To name a few: target orientation, ability to work in a team and implement organizational changes. HR must also define a remuneration system that promotes the integration process. The focus will have to be on performance as much as on how this performance was achieved.

You advise companies to proceed quickly when it comes to assessing management situations. What course of action do you suggest?
An integration project presents a golden opportunity for transparency in terms of management quality. However, such a process must be openly communicated to all those affected. A clandestine assessment and selection process will only create an atmosphere of insecurity. If this process is seen as a targeted investment in the interest of leadership development that will provide invaluable feedback for each individual's further career, it is mostly favorably received. Whatever the case may be, many successful integration managers agree that quick resolution of all leadership questions—and therefore speed—is key. Lengthy assessment and selection processes are a strain on an organization and breed feelings of insecurity.

You have mentioned the positive effects of management assessments. What about the risks?
It is more than frustrating if members of staff have to reapply for their own jobs, and such a course of action puts an employee on the spot. This is detrimental to the

entire company, especially if assessment procedures are not laid open and if feedback is obliterated. Open feedback on the other hand may trigger positive effects and motivate management and staff in general.

From an HR point of view, what are other drivers for greater integration success?
To answer this question, let us start with the so-called disaster factors, namely the reasons why an integration project fails. In my experience, the four most prominent factors for the failure of a project are: insufficient involvement of employees, an inadequate communication strategy, a focus on cost synergies instead of growth and innovation, and last, haphazard planning of the integration process.

Acquisitions are extraordinary opportunities for managers and talents alike to make their mark by taking over demanding projects and employing them for their personal development.

Key persons need to be on board as quickly as possible for them not to leave in an atmosphere of vagueness that comes with integration. The best course of action, really, is to take crucial decision makers and talents on board the core team—and speed is of the essence in this case—and motivate them to take an active stance.

Communication, communication, communication. That is what the integration phase is all about. It is for a leader to deal with, and cannot and must not be delegated. Not all the answers have to be given straight away. However, direct contact of the boss or leader of a company with their staff and entire organization has demonstrated essential in bilateral talks and town hall meetings. Communication has to flow both ways, which means that those affected can ask questions and voice their concerns in equal measure. Parallel to internal communication, communication with external contact groups such as investors, analysts, banks and the general public is just as valuable for their decisive role in judging a project a success or failure.

It is all a matter of one team, one strategy. Everyone has to know the integration targets and milestones, but also the integration project's improvement and innovation potential. Such transparency creates an atmosphere of security and motivation and commitment to meet the targets that have been set.

What relevance do you assign to intercultural differences in integration management, and how are they best dealt with?
In transnational acquisitions, sadly too little attention is usually given to aspects such as cultural differences and dissimilarities in communication. Successful integration teams are prepared to get to know those cultural differences in another organization and adapt to them accordingly instead of superimposing a new company onto another. Multicultural sensitivity and effectiveness therefore also signify that intercultural differences are purposefully utilized to create competitive advantages.

Economies of scale often induce standardization and scaling effects. Is this also true for traditional HR methods?
If a company aims for standardization, one party has to adapt, but which one? I believe it best to be guided by aspects of content, rather than stick to principles. The standardization of remuneration systems is a delicate and explosive matter, as soon as one party has to lower its sights. Common sense and a flexible approach may be rewarding, a universal approach remains but wishful thinking.

2.6 Introduce Integration Monitoring

Responsibility for the integration office is part of a company's DNA. We have amply described the roles and duties involved. This integration office role has to be lived as well; and communication breathes life to it. The topic of institutionalized integration responsibility is also part of the management's agenda; it recurs regularly on the agenda of leadership committees and can be communicated in the form of a scorecard (Fig. 2.13).

2.6.1 Integration Scorecard

Integration scorecards aim at bringing the topic of information exchange to the table of the executive management in regular intervals.[26] It is not its main goal to develop an additional complex reporting system (see Fig. 2.14), but to create an official communication format that will give integration topics heed and reiterate the company's commitment to them.

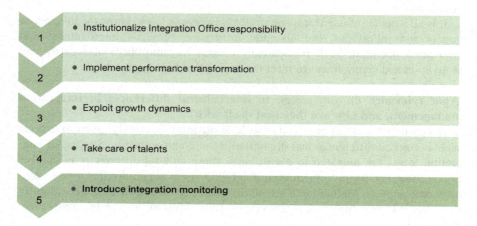

Fig. 2.13 Performance transformation concept—step 5. Source: Bergamin/Braun

---

[26]Galpin and Herndon (2000, p. 144).

2.6 Introduce Integration Monitoring

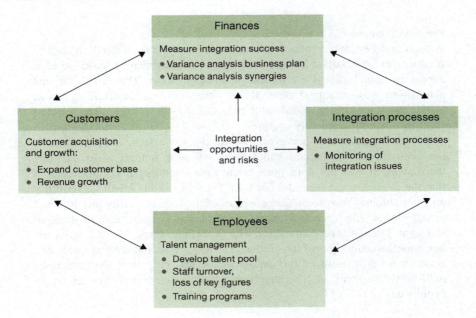

Fig. 2.14 Integration scorecard. Source: Bergamin/Braun, based on Müller-Stewens (2006, p. 16)

The scorecard comprises areas such as finances, integration processes as well as customers and employees. The following chart lists key performance indicators that seem perfectly reasonable.

Finances
- Assessment of accomplished acquisitions: variance analysis business plan versus realized figures in accomplished acquisitions (target: turnover, earnings before interest and taxes (ebit), revenue)
- Estimation of achieved synergy potentials and comparison with original targets
- Financial monitoring of selected action plans

Integration process
- Is there a vision, and how has it changed over the years?
- Adherence to individual integration plans and defined milestones
- Status report on achieved corporation-wide standardization (IT systems, branding, restructuring and distribution channels)
- Success stories

Customers
- Growth influence of previous acquisitions.
- Distribution and customer-specific impulses from previous acquisitions (cross-selling, bundling, diversification, better application of customer relationships and management of key accounts)
- Development of revenue position with the largest customers
- How many innovations have emerged through the acquired entities? Have these innovations been multiplied corporation-wide?
- Success stories

> **Practical Example**
> A food and beverage producer that predominantly concentrated on quality products and specialties in the upper-range price segment, decided to gain access to bulk business by means of an acquisition. The driver for this acquisition was—amongst other things—the board of directors that was utterly convinced of the added value potential in bulk business. The selected enterprise was subsequently acquired.
>
> It soon became clear, however, that the synergy effects and performance development that the board had banked on were not going to manifest themselves. It was not until quite some time later that it became evident that the executive manager did not back the acquisition. Albeit he skillfully and meticulously monitored the processes of the former quality provider and managed them like a micro manager, he displayed a distinct lack of strategic foresight. There was no cooperation with the acquired bulk business provider, nor were there any signs of integration. The acquired company was integrated years later, as a result of this resistance. It was only then that synergies particularly in areas such as purchasing and customer retention could be exploited.

Friction loss, non-transparency and differences in interests amongst the various executive committees of a company—between the board of directors and the executive management in the case above—are a recurring issue in daily business life. In order to nip such resistance in the bud, or better still, to make it transparent, companies are well advised to introduce integration monitoring within the framework of an integration project. This kind of monitoring can make an executive committee face up to integration intentions.

2.6.2 Opportunity and Risk Management

The scorecard is an indicator as to what opportunities and risks are likely to come up and have an impact. Risks are events, topics or areas that can hamper integration success from a corporation point of view. Opportunities on the other hand denote the yet unused potentials that present themselves in the course of performance transformation.

We refer to events as risky when they have the potential to sensitively and detrimentally affect business success whilst integration efforts are being made. Typical risks are the departure of entire management teams, a lack of corporation loyalty of certain business units, or insufficient implementation of IT systems.

Opportunities, on the other hand, refer to conditions that allow for further success potentials whilst integration efforts are being made. For example, the multiplication of existing skills in the corporation and the introduction of IT systems that boost the corporation's performance. Further opportunities are the merging of competence teams, which in turn has positive cost effects and goes hand in hand with an innovation boost. Having said that, opportunity potentials most of all imply transformative synergies.

2.6.3 Post-merger Audit

Audits are nothing out of the ordinary in many subjects. However, audits are seldom conducted during the post-merger phase. Jansen/Brügger[27] vividly encourage post-merger audits, as they are an important tool of process controlling. Financial data, and the profitability of completed transactions, plus social aspects after integration of a company regarding integration management are the subjects of investigation. We also believe that a post-integration audit of a company is a powerful tool to gauge the integration management and bring potential problems to the surface. The latter can then be the subject of debate in the corporation committees.

Companies can only benefit from identifying the areas that need to be scrutinized during a post-merger audit as soon as they start conducting an opportunity and risk analysis.

2.7 Integration Management and Performance Transformation Checklists

The following checklists illustrate at a glance what critical issues integration management needs to take into consideration. These checklists have been aligned with the different steps of the performance transformation concept. It is a step by step guide, and each step features its most relevant topics. The subsequent checklist proposes that:

- There should be an overview of all the relevant aspects of each individual step in connection with integration management.
- Companies should establish what focal points integration management has to pay attention to.
- The checklist is to be looked at as a thought-provoking impulse with respect to what other topics will have to be taken into account.

---

[27]Jansen and Brügger (2012, p. 691).

2.7.1 Checklist 2: Institutionalize Integration Office Responsibility

Checklist	Assessment		Remarks
	Not at all true	Absolutely true	
Responsibilities have been assigned Both the integration leader (who is responsible for integration success) and the integration office responsible (who supports the integration process) have been clearly communicated	① ② ③ ④ ⑤	⑥ ⑦ ⑧ ⑨ ⑩	
The determination to conduct a performance transformation (in order to attain a higher level of performance) has also been clearly communicated	① ② ③ ④ ⑤	⑥ ⑦ ⑧ ⑨ ⑩	
Legal merger aspects including their possible problem issues (competition, corporate, employment) have been identified and the respective tasks have been assigned to those in charge	① ② ③ ④ ⑤	⑥ ⑦ ⑧ ⑨ ⑩	
The institutional framework around the integration office and its responsibilities has been established; its goal has been documented and is verifiable	① ② ③ ④ ⑤	⑥ ⑦ ⑧ ⑨ ⑩	
The supporting function of the integration office responsible and their main tasks have been determined	① ② ③ ④ ⑤	⑥ ⑦ ⑧ ⑨ ⑩	
The integration leader (not the same as integration office responsibility) has been appointed and reports all integration progress to the board of directors or the executive management at regular intervals	① ② ③ ④ ⑤	⑥ ⑦ ⑧ ⑨ ⑩	
Vision, targets, milestones and synergies have been communicated clearly and their implementation is being monitored	① ② ③ ④ ⑤	⑥ ⑦ ⑧ ⑨ ⑩	

2.7.2 Checklist 3: Enforce Performance Transformation

Checklist	Assessment		Remarks
	Not at all true	Absolutely true	
Securing the pre-merger value of the existing core business	① ② ③ ④ ⑤	⑥ ⑦ ⑧ ⑨ ⑩	

(continued)

2.7 Integration Management and Performance Transformation Checklists

Determine depth of integration, i.e. autonomy versus complete integration of the target company	①	②	③	④	⑤	⑥	⑦	⑧	⑨	⑩	
Exploitation of synergy potentials, i.e. quantification and implementation monitoring	①	②	③	④	⑤	⑥	⑦	⑧	⑨	⑩	
Search for transformative synergies, i.e. radical change of status quo • IT as a lever for transformative synergies (digitization, automatization, knowledge management, etc.) • Processes as drivers of innovation (key account management, production, etc.) • Development of new business areas (diversification etc.)	①	②	③	④	⑤	⑥	⑦	⑧	⑨	⑩	

2.7.3 Checklist 4: Exploit Growth Dynamics

Checklist	Assessment										Remarks
	Not at all true					Absolutely true					
Align integration challenge with customer benefit	①	②	③	④	⑤	⑥	⑦	⑧	⑨	⑩	
Use momentum of integration process to inform and motivate staff	①	②	③	④	⑤	⑥	⑦	⑧	⑨	⑩	
Employ all communication opportunities for an initial motivational boost in the organization. Examples: • Kick-off meetings to spark the integration flame • Regular so-called town hall meetings • Walk the talk, i.e. follow your words with actions • Inform customers about their benefit and any acquisition and integration progress	①	②	③	④	⑤	⑥	⑦	⑧	⑨	⑩	
Monitor insecurities critically (e.g. staff leaving the company suddenly, customers turning to other providers)	①	②	③	④	⑤	⑥	⑦	⑧	⑨	⑩	

2.7.4 Checklist 5: Take Care of Talents

Checklist	Assessment										Remarks
	Not at all true					Absolutely true					
Due diligence of HR has been conducted	①	②	③	④	⑤	⑥	⑦	⑧	⑨	⑩	

(continued)

Checklist	Assessment	Remarks
	Not at all true — Absolutely true	
The required leadership behavior has been pinpointed and the necessary core competences have been deducted from it	① ② ③ ④ ⑤ ⑥ ⑦ ⑧ ⑨ ⑩	
Management assessments are being conducted. Important: • Selection and assessment process according to the core competences mentioned above • These assessments must be followed by feedback	① ② ③ ④ ⑤ ⑥ ⑦ ⑧ ⑨ ⑩	
Make rapid leadership decisions, e.g.: • Appoint CEO, CFO and other key persons • Devise action plans for unforeseen and unwanted HR developments to be able to react swiftly	① ② ③ ④ ⑤ ⑥ ⑦ ⑧ ⑨ ⑩	
Personnel development, e.g.: • Clarify terms and conditions for key persons (i.e. contract, relocation, questions of logistics)	① ② ③ ④ ⑤ ⑥ ⑦ ⑧ ⑨ ⑩	
Are there sufficient resources for the planned integration efforts?	① ② ③ ④ ⑤ ⑥ ⑦ ⑧ ⑨ ⑩	
Promote learning processes between buying company and target organization, e.g.: • Deployment policy • Vital integration committees are composed in equal part • Stimulate learning processes • Communication flows both ways • Scrutinize standardization of HR processes and enforce those processes purposefully	① ② ③ ④ ⑤ ⑥ ⑦ ⑧ ⑨ ⑩	
Introduce reward systems that account for the integration targets	① ② ③ ④ ⑤ ⑥ ⑦ ⑧ ⑨ ⑩	

2.7.5 Checklist 6: Introduce Integration Monitoring

Checklist	Assessment		Remarks
	Not at all true	Absolutely true	
The reporting of the integration management is proving effective. Crucial conditions are being fulfilled e.g. concerning: • Reporting template • Reporting intervals • Recipients of reporting	① ② ③ ④ ⑤	⑥ ⑦ ⑧ ⑨ ⑩	

(continued)

The reporting of the integration management addresses the most pressing problem issues, e.g.: • Finances • Customers • Staff • Integration processes	①	②	③	④	⑤	⑥	⑦	⑧	⑨	⑩
Wholehearted acceptance of reporting by: • Management • Board of directors • Executive management	①	②	③	④	⑤	⑥	⑦	⑧	⑨	⑩
Reporting has revealed to be effective and addresses the most pressing integration topics. Problem issues such as non- transparency between or amongst the committees, lack of openness, conflicts of interest are being paid enough attention to	①	②	③	④	⑤	⑥	⑦	⑧	⑨	⑩
The opportunity and risk assessment during the integration process has been conducted and has brought the most vital aspects to light	①	②	③	④	⑤	⑥	⑦	⑧	⑨	⑩
Post-merger audits are being conducted and openly provide information about integration progress	①	②	③	④	⑤	⑥	⑦	⑧	⑨	⑩

2.8 Legal Aspects of Post-merger Integrations

By Petra Hanselmann
lic.iur., LL.M., Attorney at law, Partner, Baker McKenzie Zurich

The value realized in an acquisition depends to a large extent on the ability of the buyer to successfully integrate the acquired business into its own organization. Key drivers for integration are the strategic and operational reasoning behind the transaction as well as the determination of tax risks and tax planning opportunities. However, in order to successfully implement the desired structure, a number of legal aspects need to be taken into consideration. The following is a limited selection of legal topics frequently dealt with in multinational integration processes.

2.8.1 Due Diligence

The acquiring company should perform a legal due diligence with regard to the entities involved in post-acquisition integration in order to identify any potential legal issues that might affect the integration process. The due diligence should not be limited to the acquired entities being integrated, but instead also encompass the buyer's existing entities. Ideally, integration issues should already be part of the acquisition due diligence process. Not only would this be more cost effective, but it could also help to overcome the inherent problems associated with collecting information for the integration process once the acquisition has been completed.

When acquiring a competitor, exchanging information during the due diligence process and in the period between signing until completion of the transaction needs to be managed specifically and monitored closely. Commercial and competition law can influence the exchange of information among competitors. From a commercial perspective, the seller on the one hand wants to limit its liability from a breach of representation and warranties by making extensive disclosure in the due diligence; on the other hand, the seller needs to limit disclosure in order to protect their business in case the transaction is not completed. From a competition law perspective, it is essential that the parties remain in full competition until the transaction has been successfully completed and, thus, abstain from exchanging sensitive information (for further details, see Sect. 8.2).

2.8.2 Competition Law Aspects

A suspension period must often be observed between signing and closing of an acquisition, for example, because merger control approvals need to be obtained or other conditions to closing need to be fulfilled. However, the buyer is usually eager to start planning the post-closing integration process as soon as the signing has occurred in order to complete the integration process as early as possible. This constellation raises issues that must be carefully considered in the context of the integration planning process so as to avoid any competition law issues.

Merger control laws usually require parties to suspend the closing and the implementation of a transaction until the necessary merger approvals are available or until the respective waiting periods have expired. Violating the respective merger control laws may lead to fines. While the parties can essentially begin the integration planning in the period between signing and closing, they should strictly avoid any acts that could be considered an implementation of the transaction during this period.

As mentioned above, if the parties are competitors, it is important to ensure that the exchange of information during the due diligence and until the closing of the transaction complies with applicable competition laws. For this purpose, information is often divided into three different categories:

a. *Permitted information*

Data that is aggregated, historic (i.e. more than one year old) or already in the public domain, such as published financial statements or the corporate structure of the target, can generally be freely transferred among the parties.

2.8 Legal Aspects of Post-merger Integrations

b. *Restricted information*

Depending on the specific circumstances, it might be possible to exchange certain sensitive information such as historic (i.e. more than one year old) individual (i.e. non-aggregated) product margin information with a limited number of individuals for the purposes of the integration process.

c. *Prohibited information*

The exchange of sensitive information such as pricing data, customer information, or future pricing intentions among competitors before the closing of the transaction constitutes a violation of competition laws.

To address the fact that certain sensitive information cannot be exchanged among competitors until the transaction has been completed, and as such data might be important for the integration process, it has become increasingly common to delegate the review of such sensitive information to independent consultants or legal counsels. These independent third parties review the data and prepare a report which does not contain sensitive information (for example, by aggregating data). Often, parties also set up so-called "clean teams", which consist of a limited number of party employees that are not involved in the day-to-day business of the involved companies. From a competition law perspective, these clean teams may—subject to strict confidentiality obligations—review sensitive information for the purpose of planning the integration process.[28]

The three categories described above are general guidelines only and the exchange of data and information in a transaction before closing always depends on the particular industry and the specific facts and individual circumstances of a transaction.

2.8.3 Corporate Law Aspects

Integration processes frequently involve mergers of acquired subsidiaries with the buyer's existing local subsidiaries. Many jurisdictions have statutory merger procedures in place that allow an automatic transfer of assets, liabilities and contracts. Most of these jurisdictions also have a short-form statutory merger procedure that is less complicated and cheaper to implement than the ordinary merger procedure. However, these short-form merger procedures are typically only available for a parent-subsidiary or brother-sister merger. In order to benefit from short-form merger procedures in the integration process, it might be advisable, as a pre-integration step, to create a share ownership structure where the dissolving subsidiaries are direct subsidiaries of or sister companies with the entity into which they will be merged.

In jurisdictions that do not have a merger statute, an asset transfer followed by liquidation of the transferring entity might be required to achieve the desired

---

[28]See Sect. 4.3 for clean teams used in the LafargeHolcim integration process.

integration and reduction of the number of entities. An individual asset transfer might also be required if only part of the business of an entity is to be transferred to another entity. In individual asset transfers, specific steps often need to be observed in order to transfer legal ownership of assets to the acquiring entity. The steps required depend on the kind of assets transferred and the jurisdiction involved. The transfer of legal title in real estate, for example, often needs to be registered with the competent local authorities to become effective.

In an individual asset transfer, additional steps are required for the transfer of contracts when compared with the statutory merger processes in which contracts are generally automatically transferred by law to the surviving entity. Generally, either a notice of assignment needs to be given to the counterparty or specific consent from the other party to the transfer of the contract needs to be obtained. Contracts might also contain so-called "change of control" clauses that trigger the counterparty's termination rights as a consequence of the merger or the asset transfer. Thus, contracts should be reviewed in advance of an intended transfer or merger so as to determine whether such contracts are freely transferable or if the consent of the other party is required, particularly if important contracts are to be transferred as part of the integration process.

Integrations often involve transactions that require specific corporate approvals. Therefore, it is always advisable to timely consult applicable local law and the relevant constitutional documents of the involved entities to determine whether there are any specific restrictions from a corporate law perspective. Depending on the jurisdiction, corporate actions (such as required amendments to constitutional documents or the adoption of board or shareholder resolutions) might be time consuming and should therefore be addressed early in the integration process.

Key employees of the acquired entities frequently leave after the completion of an acquisition. Often, these key employees also function as officers or directors of the entities involved in the integration process or act as resident shareholders. If key employees terminate their employment after the acquisition, it is important to (i) timely replace these employees as officers or directors in the respective entities if this is required for the entities to be able to take the necessary corporate actions in connection with the integration process, and (ii) make sure that the employees sign the necessary documents in connection with their residential shareholder position before they leave the company, as it might be difficult to locate them afterwards to sign the required transfer documents.

2.8.4 Employment Law Aspects

In many jurisdictions, particularly in the EU and Switzerland, employees pertaining to a business are automatically transferred by law in an asset transfer consisting of a business or part thereof. The same applies in a statutory merger. In other jurisdictions, employees are not automatically transferred in a business transfer but their contracts need to be terminated and they need to be rehired. Furthermore, in a merger or business transfer, many jurisdictions have obligations to inform and potentially consult employees or employee representatives prior to the merger or business transfer. The duration of the information and consultation process depends on the jurisdiction and might have a timing impact on the integration process. The consequences of failing to inform or consult also depend on the jurisdiction. In certain jurisdictions, for example, financial penalties are imposed for failing to consult or inform; in other jurisdictions, the transfer can be considered void.

As part of the post-merger integration process, the buyer is often eager to harmonize the terms and conditions of acquired employees with those of existing employees. In many jurisdictions, however, employees are protected from changes to their working conditions, which limits the extent to which such harmonization can be implemented in an integration process without employee consent.

After an acquisition, the acquiring company might also plan to downsize its workforce. Redundancies and mass dismissals might be required. Depending on the jurisdiction, specific consultation procedures and other legal restrictions need to be observed, which might have a major impact on the integration process.

2.8.5 Conclusion

In multinational integration projects, the legal peculiarities of the various jurisdictions involved need to be identified and addressed early in the integration process in order to avoid any unexpected implementation and timing issues. Human resource aspects, corporate issues, regulatory approval and filing requirements in particular, often have a major impact on timing. When acquiring a competitor, compliance with applicable competition laws is essential.

The integration process usually imposes a substantial additional workload on the employees of the involved entities besides the ordinary day-to-day business. External lawyers are thus often engaged for legal aspects of post-merger projects. However, internal employees are usually the best source of information. For an efficient integration process it is therefore important that outside counsels and internal employees work closely together to best exploit internal knowhow and an outside counsel's expertise.

References

Bucerius, M. (2004). Post-Merger-Integration: Typische Gestaltungsformen und ihre Erfolgsauswirkungen. *M&A-Review*, 12.

DePamphilis, D. (2003). *Mergers, acquisitions, and other restructuring activities*. Millbrae, CA: Academic Press.

Deutsch, C., & West, A. (2010). *A new generation of M&A: A McKinsey perspective on the opportunities and challenges*. McKinsey & Company, Perspectives on merger integration, June.

Fuhrer, C. A. (2007). *Akquisitions- und Integrationsmanagement: Wie können Kompetenzen erfolgreich integriert und neuer Wertschöpfung zugeführt werden?* Dissertation, Hochschulschrift Universität St. Gallen.

Galpin, T. J., & Herndon, M. (2000). *Complete guide to mergers and acquisitions.* San Francisco: Jossey-Bass, A Wiley Company.

Gerds, J., & Schewe, G. (2014). Post merger integration: Unternehmenserfolg durch integration excellence (5. Auflage). Berlin: Springer Verlag.

Gupta, A., Stephenson, T., & West, A. (2010). *Integrating sales operations in a merger: A McKinsey perspective on four essential steps.* McKinsey & Company, Perspectives on merger integration, June 2010.

Habeck, M. M. (2013). *Frohn Fabian; Walleyo, Samy: Fusionsfieber 2.0: Wie man eher, schneller und nachhaltiger bei Übernahmen Erfolge erzielt.* Wiesbaden: Springer Fachmedien Verlag.

Hackmann, S. (2011). *Organisatorische Gestaltung in der Post Merger Integration: eine organisationstheoretische Betrachtung unterschiedlicher Integrationsansätze.* Dissertation Universität Giessen, Gabler Verlag, Wiesbaden.

Haspeslagh, P. C., & Jemison, D. B. (1992). *Akquisitionsmanagement: Wertschöpfung durch strategische Neuausrichtung des Unternehmens.* Frankfurt: Campus Verlag.

Jansen, S. A., & Brügger, C. (2012). Integrationsmanagement bei Unternehmenszusammenschlüssen. In G. Picot (Hrsg.), *Handbuch mergers and acquisitions: Planung – Durchführung – Integration* (5. Auflage). Stuttgart: Schäffer-Poeschel Verlag.

McLetchie, J. (2010). *Next-generation integration management office: A McKinsey perspective on organizing integrations to create value.* McKinsey & Company, Perspectives on merger integration, June 2010.

McLetchie, J., & West, A. (2010). *Beyond risk avoidance: A McKinsey perspective on creating tranformational value from mergers.* McKinsey & Company, Perspectives on merger integration, June 2010.

Müller-Stewens, G. (2006). Konzeptionelle Entscheidungen beim Post-Merger-Management. In B. H. Wirtz (Hrsg.), *Handbuch Mergers & Acquisitions Management.* Wiesbaden: Gabler Verlag.

Müller-Stewens, G. (2010). Konzeptionelle Organisationen. In G. Müller-Stewens, S. Kunisch, & A. Binder (Hrsg.), *Mergers and Acquisitions: Analysen, Trends und Best Practices.* Stuttgart: Schäffer-Poeschel Verlag.

Müller-Stewens, G., Kunisch, S., & Binder, A. (Hrsg.) (2010). Mergers & Acquisitions: Analysen, Trends und Best Practices. Stuttgart: Schäffer-Poeschel Verlag.

Schreiner, A., Wirth, M., & Wirth, T. (2010). From Good to Great – Erfolgsfaktoren aus der Praxis in der Umsetzung aus Verkäuferperspektive. In G. Müller-Stewens, S. Kunisch, & A. Binder (Hrsg.), *Mergers and acquisitions: Analysen, Trends und Best Practices.* Stuttgart: Schäffer-Poeschel Verlag.

Sprenger, R. K. (2012). *Radikal Führen.* Frankfurt: Campus Verlag.

Unger, M. (2007). *Handbuch Mergers & Acquisitions.* Wien: Linde.

Global Merger *dormakaba*: Interview and Case Study

3

Kaba, provider of security and access solutions (listed), and Dorma, provider of door technology systems and services (family business) merged in 2015. The new company, dormakaba—after acquisitions in North America—has a turnover of CHF 2.7 billion for the financial year 2016/2017 and is the new global number 2 with 18,000 employees in over 50 countries.

The merger represents one of the most complex mergers in Swiss industrial history. The Group has its headquarters in Switzerland and is listed at the SIX Swiss Exchange. Listed dormakaba Holding AG owns a controlling share of 52.2%, whereas the former owners of Dorma own a share of 47.5% of the combined operative business. The main shareholders on both sides have committed to a long-term pool contract, which safeguards shareholder continuity.

Dorma with its headquarters in Ennepetal near Dusseldorf/Germany, and Kaba, headquartered in Rümlang/Switzerland, largely complement each other in terms of product range, their position in the construction cycle as well as their market presence in Asia-Pacific and America. Both companies have an excellent presence in Europe, while Dorma is rather more strongly represented in the Asia-Pacific region, and Kaba is more anchored in America.

The integration project has been up and running for the last 2 years along the principle of "only the best will do for the new". Substantial integration questions have already been resolved or are being implemented, respectively. It would be premature to judge the merger as a whole a success or a failure, albeit its outlook is certainly positive. However, a look at how well the integration management has fared to this date will undoubtedly be interesting. The following is an interview with Riet Cadonau, CEO of dormakaba.

3.1 Interview with Riet Cadonau, CEO dormakaba Group

What are the experiences and conclusions from project planning and the first phase of this project, over 365 days after the closing of a global merger? What went according to plan? What surprises and major challenges emerged?

Riet Cadonau meticulously studied merger projects of a similar scale, such as Novaris, ABB or LafargeHolcim and applied his knowledge to the integration efforts from day one. dormakaba's goal and prudent decision to start their integration management very early on helped their key committees to proactively and thoroughly acquaint themselves with the target structure. A mere 4 months after the transaction, the new group management was able to present their future operating model, a concept that was implemented zealously by the entire organization 6 months later.

The dormakaba merger followed a stringent timeline that was communicated straightforward internally to provide employees with a sense of process security during a time of uncertainty.

- April 30, 2015: announcement of the merger
- May 22, 2015: extraordinary general assembly
- July 2, 2015: announcement of the new group management
- July–October, 2015: establishment of a new operating model, workshops with the group management and at a later stage with 100 key persons of the group, with subsequent communication of the new organization
- September 1, 2015: closing
- January 4, 2016: Organization Day. All relevant organizational and HR questions have been made
- July 1, 2016: Day One. Go live with the new target organization and processes accordingly, as well as start of roll-out of the new umbrella brand *dormakaba*

At the time of the interview, the integration process is proceeding according to the defined schedule. The costs for the merger that were communicated when it was announced have increased due to extraordinary expenses. After validation of the integration projects, a more substantial shift in high-price countries occurred than originally anticipated. Cadonau describes the significantly increased workload and coping with it as one of the main challenges for the organization on the whole and the management in particular.

3.2 Our First Hypothesis: Integration Planning Starts as Early as During the M&A Transaction Phase Before the Closing

It is never too early to initiate integration activities.
Philip Robinson, Stefan Rösch-Rütsche, Samy Walleyo (EY)

3.2 Our First Hypothesis: Integration Planning Starts as Early as During the M

When did you start integration planning with dormakaba, and how did you proceed? What were your priorities and what principles did you follow?

dormakaba took charge of integration planning—as far as possible within the legal framework—even before the closing. Integration planning represented an integral part of the dormakaba transaction process. No integration planning meant there would be no approval of the transaction, neither by the group management nor the board, says Riet Cadonau.

The post-merger integration management of dormakaba is based on three pillars:

- Core projects: Infrastructure projects, e.g. reporting, information systems
- Value driver initiatives: Business plan relevant projects
- Change management: How should the process of change be managed; how should cultural differences be addressed?

Speed in HR decisions is of the essence and was therefore one of the top priorities. Haste, however, must not mar quality. Therefore, assessments of key persons were conducted as early as straight after closing. These assessments followed a distinct pattern; decision makers in both companies independently formed their opinion of the candidates in question. An external team of experts formed part of this evaluation process to ensure a professional assessment procedure. This external team also took part in the meetings of the nomination committee.

The principle of "only the best will do for the new" was stringently applied too when nominating the top management, as it was commonly acknowledged that the right personalities and the management team as a unit were crucial for success. Every position deserved only the best candidate. Ambiguous leadership situations, such as e.g. co-management solutions, were relinquished, as they lead to leadership confusion and create an atmosphere of insecurity. Rapid decision-taking also aimed to shorten the time of uncertainty for individual members of the management as much as possible.

Additional focus was placed on labeling and quantifying synergy effects proactively. Top-down targets with respect to synergy benefits set clear goals and are a driver, also because employees accepted the merger as being industrially logical in general and therefore good news.

How detailed was your integration planning? What were your experiences with respect to integration plan adaptation and implementation difficulties and opposition?

Meticulous integration planning is key to successful accomplishment. The more intricate, the more important the validation from below. dormakaba employs toolkits and dashboards as reporting instruments. Each project has clearly defined milestones with a carefully appointed project accountable ("responsibility has a first and a last name") and allocated resources. Milestones are clearly communicated and the focus then lies on their implementation. Early communication creates process security.

According to Cadonau, clearly communicated goals and processes are also critical when it comes to adapting plans or if there are implementation issues, as in synergy plans, for instance. Any fine-tuning of cuts is almost inexorably met with opposition, if the new detailed planning does not comprehensively match previous expectations. In such cases, local units may rebuff the new targets as extortionate and react with disbelief and indignation.

The dormakaba management has anticipated such reactions, and has decided that targets on a group level are to be set before the fine-tuning of synergy projects. The distribution of targets and synergy sources may be adapted. As a result, group targets can be maintained and business units will still be at liberty to individually plan their implementation and share the responsibility.

Plans and their implementation are coordinated centrally via the Integration Management Office (IMO), there are thus so-called change requests for cases as described above.

3.3 Our Second Hypothesis: Project Management Skills Are Central to Successful Integration Management, i.e. Top-level Guiding Coalitions, an Integration Road Map and Clear Responsibilities

What conclusions have you drawn from project management during the integration phase? What challenges do you anticipate when confronted with other cultures and mentalities?

dormakaba applies its project management methods uniformly, not just to the integration project dormakaba itself. These methods apply to IT projects, reorganizations, but also to M&A transactions and subsequent integration. This way, the usual PMI planning (post-merger integration) is always part of the acquisition proposal to the board of directors. No acquisition decision is ever taken without clear PMI outlines. This merger was no exception to the rule.

dormakaba works along a unified PMI concept. The receiving unit, i.e. the buyer segment and their segment leader carry the integration responsibility and as a rule chairs the steering committee. The segment leader is the promoter of the acquisition decision and subsequent integration at the same time. CEO and CFO are on the superordinate sounding board, which allows them to monitor the situation and intervene should they detect any deviations from the schedule (Fig. 3.1).

Cadonau puts great emphasis on the fact that business is in the hands of the local management. True to the motto of checks and balances, however, the person responsible for finance for the acquired company is recruited from the ranks of dormakaba. Right from the beginning dormakaba appoints a PMI manager who will then spend the next 12 months on-site to ensure that dormakaba's own PMI concept is implemented. Regular development reports have to be presented to the management during this time in order to assess the relationship of integration project and business plan.

3.3 Our Second Hypothesis: Project Management Skills Are Central to Successful...

Fig. 3.1 Standard PMI organization at dormakaba. Source: Bergamin/Braun

The processes, structures and principles mentioned above can all be found in the integration project of the dormakaba merger. With the exception that in connection with the merger, dormakaba on a group level employs staff who deal with integration management on a full-time basis. They form the so-called Integration Management Office (IMO). They are assisted by full-time peers in the segments and in group functions. The build-up of capacities in the integration management allows dormakaba to let their segments devote themselves to the principle of "customer first". Their staff in sales and operations should be unreservedly devoted to their customers. The integration management responsibilities, in contrast, are in the hands of the Integration Management Office and the designated persons in the segments and group functions, as well as the management. This clear-cut binary division of responsibilities has so far enabled dormakaba to implement its integration project professionally and reveal good business results at the same time.

The benefits of a structured and systematic course of action with clear responsibilities are obvious. Where do you see the challenges in project management, especially in dealing with other cultural backgrounds and mentalities?

Communication and dialogue is pivotal. Riet Cadonau stresses the importance of a local presence with an impact. He and his group management colleagues therefore regularly visit customers and partners all over the world, subsidiaries included, and keep in touch with staff. Communication is central. You have to be able to not only send information, but also to receive it. Looking back over the last 5 years, and assessing his own skills in that matter, his personal progress allows him to now open meetings with a range of open questions. This greatly encourages a feedback process that reveals where the shoe in the organization does not fit.

The same holds true for project management: communication is a key instrument alongside clear goals, processes, structures and the definition of responsibilities. As in the superordinate integration project, all projects below are critically influenced by a mutual, common understanding and ongoing dialogue. The challenge is to stop and behold in a dynamic and rapidly changing environment in order to accomplish this basic work and by doing so set the foundations for a successful project.

3.4 Our Third Hypothesis: Measures in Integration Management Depend on Each Individual Case and Are a Matter of Common Sense and Sound Judgement. Employing Synergies Effectively Requires Professional Change Management

How do you proceed when scaling integration measures? What guidelines do you follow?

Clearly defined financial goals are imperative. Targets must be broken down to the segment level and group functions. Moreover, projects have to be bulletproof against both a business assessment and resources planning. The core question is whether projects can be managed with the allocated resources, or whether business will suffer as a result of them.

Bilanz[1] concludes that after the merger there are still two operative units "dorma" and "kaba" active in the market. What motivated this decision?

Riet Cadonau disagrees. The two former organizations were merged on an operational level, strictly so since July 1, 2016, i.e. 10 months after closing. The company is undergoing an adaptation, which means a standardization and simplification of its legal structure. Close to 200 legal entities mean a considerable time-investment. The same holds for the adjustment of the market structure. dormakaba is being implemented as the umbrella brand, which, however, is a medium-term project, not least due to the fact that the brand value of each individual brand must be retained when transferred to the new umbrella brand.

What significance do you attribute to the principle of simplicity?

Structures, processes, concepts and communication should be as transparent and straightforward as possible. dormakaba's mission is that "we make access in life smart and secure". Smart also means simple and customer-friendly. One of the most important out of our five company values is "customer first", which means that employees, customers, investors should experience any sort of exchange or contact as utterly simple and hassle-free.

How do you deal with change management? What particular changes do you see with other business cultures?

Change management is one of the three pillars of the PMI concept, which only emphasizes the importance of this aspect for successful integration.

Riet Cadonau believes that change management is as important as management alignment and leadership conduct. The following are his leadership principles.

Leaders must:

- Act as role models and practice as they preach,
- Actively demonstrate customer orientation and propagate it,
- Promote competent and committed employees,

---

[1]Bilanz (20/2016, pp. 46–50): "dormakaba: Mit Haken und Ösen" (English: "dormakaba, the arduous way to the dream marriage").

- Listen before they decide, and once a decision has been taken, focus on its stringent implementation.

Goals and a good plan are central. If there are bridges to gap with respect to achieving objectives, they are to be addressed swiftly and adequately.

The following lists some of the tools that dormakaba successfully used in the change process:

- Pulse checks: Regular pulse checks are conducted on around 2000 employees so as to assess the current atmosphere in the organization. This quickly reveals any feelings of discontent, insecurity, listlessness etc. to allow those in charge to react promptly.
- "Activate dormakaba": This term denotes a combination of workshops, trainings, and further target-oriented communication activities that should acquaint all staff with the so-called big picture—ambition, mission, values, brand and strategy as well as business-relevant growth drivers, priorities and plans.
- Workshops and leadership trainings: These trainings focus on change management. It is the be-all and end-all of dealing with different business cultures as well as daily business, to raise awareness for discrepancies and keep them in sight. A course in leadership training, for instance, has been devised that exclusively addresses change management and intercultural challenges.
- On-site communication and electronic aids: The group management is constantly on the move and believes in what they refer to as "walk the talk". So-called townhall meetings are made transparent in the monthly group management meetings. Apart from the intranet, dormakaba uses Yammer (enterprise social networking service for private communication within organizations) as their communication tool. Cadonau had his reservations initially, but a year on, experiences are positive. Employees of the organization use the Yammer platform to post information about their projects, share experiences and celebrate success stories. This exchange keeps people in touch and encourages the company's team spirit globally.
- Emotions and personal encounters are essential during the process of change. Cadonau thus motivates staff to take part in company events. The company invites a comparatively high number of employees to visit the dormakaba stand at trade fairs. It greatly encourages the exchange of information and at the same time promotes a feeling of oneness with the company and its spirit of optimism. In the name of exchange promotion, Cadonau has decided not to scrutinize his employee's travel expenses during the first 2 years after the merger. From his point of view, it is important to encourage such an exchange.

Hans Hess maintains that effective synergy management relies on a mutual understanding of all cooperation partners. What is your view?

> The actual and sustainable benefit of an M&A transaction will only manifest itself, if customers, employees and investors are able to thoroughly understand its purpose and ultimately embrace it.
>
> Hans Hess, President of Swissmem (Association MEM Industries), Chairman and member of the Board of various Swiss industrial enterprises.

Only if employees have thoroughly understood the purpose of an M&A transaction can change be embraced. It is ultimately the condition for a successful merger. The strategic fit is indispensable—and dormakaba undoubtedly had it; complementarity of its products (around 80%), as well as in its positioning in Asia and America, and with respect to the construction cycle: Dorma has a stronger presence in new building construction, Kaba, on the other hand, is more focused on the management of the installed basis.

A mutual understanding of all cooperation partners is essential and should start as early as the groundwork itself. The merger of dormakaba put great emphasis on listening to each other, and readiness to learn from the start. At the beginning, there were no preconceptions with respect to what the results should or could be. Empathy and the ability to listen built the basis for the teams to work on solutions for the future. These encounters and workshops gradually led to the formation of guiding coalitions.

This approach was first applied amongst the eleven members of the group management, who met in four workshops of 4 days each over a period of 3 months after the extraordinary general meeting had given its approval. The preliminary aim was to create a solid basis for future cooperation and to get to know each other not as leaders and experts but as genuine human beings.

As an example, Cadonau refers to the establishment of the new operating model, which was developed in the workshops mentioned above. To begin with, the aim was to understand the partner's business model, as only a detailed knowledge of your partner will create the necessary conditions for the development of any future operating model. They ventured into a greenfield approach and always strictly adhered to the principle of "only the best will do for the new". The development and communication of the new operating model (including the new roles and principles) and the selection of the new management down to country level were central aspects. Once the operating model had its blueprint, it was presented to and discussed with the upper management of around one hundred managers within the dormakaba Group.

Chinese investors often think in terms of winner-loser categories. Change management aims for win-win situations, which may contrast with longstanding traditions. What are your experiences with Asian mentality? Are the Chinese more likely to leave things to the local management, or do they rather take an active stance in integration management? Are they reluctant to change or are they open for it?

Cadonau claims that there is no such thing as Asian mentality as a whole. There are fundamental differences between the North of China, Hong Kong and Singapore. Asian culture distinguishes itself by its immense diversity. It is always important not to lose face. Asian partners need a platform to express themselves and prefer open questions to voice their opinions and considerations. As mentioned before, sending and receiving information may not always yield congruent results. For this reason, Cadonau asks for a conversation or talk to be summarized and then explicitly gets his interlocutor's approval (congruence of sending and receiving).

dormakaba is represented in China by several thousand staff and thereby primarily trusts its local management that has a vast experience in working within Western companies and has partly been trained in Western countries. Such competence is instrumental in bridging gaps between different cultures.

Overall, Asiatic regions revealed an open and positive stance in all matters integration and were quick to implement measures; possibly due to the fact that the excellent strategic fit had generated a climate of acceptance for the merger.

How was the new unit organized and how were synergies put to use?

The merged dormakaba consists of six business segments, whereby the four access solutions segments are tightly connected with one another and sport a high degree of integration. The remaining two business units (key systems and movable walls, respectively) are independent, global businesses with a low degree of integration.

The access solutions segment features eight global product clusters:

- Door hardware
- Entrance systems
- Electronic access and data
- Services
- Master key systems
- Lodging systems
- Safe locks
- Interior glass systems

These global product clusters are managed by the regions Americas, EMEA, DACH and APAC within the framework of a matrix organization. Each segment is responsible for their individual products. The market and country segments are organized according to one of five archetypes to ensure consistent points of intersection. Group functions such as IT, legal procurement and HR are governed centrally. Cadonau is ostensibly delighted that the two independent segments, movable walls and key systems made their substantial contributions during the merger. They voluntarily took over elements of the new operating model, which sent ripples of learning achievements throughout the entire company.

So far, synergies have been largely achieved from cost cuts, for instance as a result of a consolidation of infrastructure as well as procurement. First customer decisions based on the "all from one hand" approach, however, are already proof of the merger's strategic fit.

3.5 Our Fourth Hypothesis: Speed Is of the Essence when It Comes to Appointing Key Positions or Outlining the New Organization

What are your experiences regarding this principle of speed? In your opinion, how decisive are other business cultures?

A merger such as dormakaba unsettles both partners' historical structures. Acquisitions are daily business for many managers, a merger on the other hand often represents a singular project in their careers. Cadonau stresses the importance of process security during the integration phase. The climate of uncertainty demands rapid decisions in all matters concerning the top management and the organization. This phase of vagueness must be kept as short as possible, a guideline that applies to all cultures. As mentioned before, key decision makers have to be consulted early on and they must be involved into the decision-making process. Once the management has been aligned, changes have to be implemented rapidly and consistently. dormakaba announced its top management (group management) about 2 months after the merger was communicated (April 30, 2015) and before the closing (September 1, 2015). The appointment of the group management was the basis for all decisions on the next management levels.

Cultural differences are to be respected, of course. Sweden, for example is consensus-driven; whereas the Chinese have to be invited to give their opinion without making them lose face. Alongside these regional cultural differences, there are business cultures that prefer a central approach, some again are rather in favor of more decentralization.

What is your opinion on the following? Speed and flexibility are key factors in the transformation process, which can be an issue when it comes to Asia.

Cadonau agrees that speed is crucial. Yet, rapid implementation requires an achievable plan. Adherence to clearly defined milestones averts insecurity within the organization. Flexibility, openness and an interest in dealing with something new and different are indispensable. dormakaba's principle of "only the best will do for the new" too is based on openness. Integration in the Asia-Pacific region is right on track in this sense.

3.6 Our Fifth Hypothesis: Sufficient and Suitable Personnel Resources Have a Considerable Impact on Sustainable Integration Success. Top Performers Ensure that there Is a Talent Pool to Resort to for Large Projects

What are the relevant aspects of people management in international integration projects? How can you build a talent pool that meets the demands of large global projects?

On a group level, dormakaba has available talented employees who work in integration management full-time. Ideally, 40 is the average age of staff in the integration pool and according PMI project teams; they are generalists as well as experts with development potential. CEOs must consciously invest in integration management resources. By doing do, they are fully aware of a temporary increase in costs, with the benefit, however, that the majority of staff can continue to dedicate themselves to their customers and "keep their eyes on the ball", in a manner of speaking, dormakaba's mantra. All too often, the operative business suffers in post-merger situations.

To commit talents to the new company who are not involved in PMI integration, key persons were identified in all segments and functions. They were promptly offered attractive perspectives.

Conflict management: What typical conflict situations has dormakaba experienced and how were they addressed?

The integration process is about merging two different companies into one new organization. Interests and views may clash when it comes to fusing two organizations into one. Nominating the key positions of course initially created an environment of insecurity.

The establishment of new reporting lines, processes and locations, or the harmonization of management levels and remuneration and bonus systems, as well as the mere difference in cultures may cause dissent.

Despite the time constraints and pressing integration matters, the management is well advised to pay sufficient heed to conflict management.

The remuneration and bonus system sparked intense discussions at dormakaba. One side historically issued disproportionately high wages and below average bonuses, whereas the new set up provides an average basic salary, a short-term performance-related cash bonus and a long-term variable share-based compensation. The system needed diligent explanation; one core message was that an above average income is guaranteed following a successful business performance, the payout on the other hand would be lower. This system clearly reveals its business orientation.

The introduction of new roles almost invariably entails discussions. Cadonau recalls that the role of Chief Technology Officer (CTO) introduced some years earlier had first raised eyebrows with former Kaba. It took 2 years before the new function was understood and accepted throughout the organization. Today, the CTO function has become an integral part of the company, and the CTO is part of the group management. The CTO plays an instrumental role in the Group's digitization strategy by driving projects such as the introduction of cloud-based solutions (disruptive technologies). The CTO equally partakes in the due diligence process that is conducted with M&A transactions.

3.7 Conflict Management During the Integration Process

Where in integration management does conflict typically arise and how can it be resolved? Conflict management presents a major challenge in integration management. This section thus examines the reasons for conflict and illustrates possible solutions to resolve it. The following chart is based on the authors' own experiences and features additional expert feedback (Fig. 3.2).

Conflict Management in Mergers & Acquisitions

Types of and reasons for conflict

Economic changes (redistribution or alteration of economic rewards)
- Individual **finance** issues (salaries, reward systems, travel expenses etc.)
- Organizational resources (technologies, training, **office** support etc.)

Organizational changes (change in power structure)
- Leadership (management positions, leadership culture)
- Nomination of positions
- Limited resources (people with different priorities vying for the same resources will inevitably clash)
- Organizational process (reduction of direct control due to centralization, changing reporting relationships)
- Locations (culture, language, regulations etc.)

Process changes
- Process landscape including tools/systems (best of both worlds)
- Individual routines (**modified** reporting methods, daily processes, increasing workload)
- Cultural changes
- Different cultures and values (people aspect)
- Making sense of organizational change (change management)
- Differences in convictions can be a source of **conflict** and misunderstandings
- A lack of understanding of what the other party does
- Miscommunication and personality differences

Emotional reactions
- Fear and uncertainty
- Respect (for the company, employees, managers of the acquired company)
- Pressure (deadlines)

Impact & Measures in order to manage conflicts

Impacts of destructive conflict and behavioral disintegration in teams
- Slowed down integration of the companies
- Competitors will begin to lure away talented employees
- Success of the merger is put in jeopardy

Measures to manage conflict
- Leadership teams need to be able to create a climate that promotes an open and honest discussion of issues ("tone at the top").
- They need to develop new attitudes towards **conflict**, develop trust among team members, work collaboratively, and enhance the emotional intelligence of the team.
- Team members ensure that things stay on track by applying constructive communication techniques such as listening carefully, sharing thoughts and feelings, and collaborating to develop creative solutions to problems.
- Implement processes that allow employees to voice their opinions and be heard. It is crucial that employees become more than mere recipients of communication by giving them the opportunity to share their feedback concerning the integration process.
- Create a new task on which employees from both the acquiring and acquired company work together.
- The creation of a new task will prevent employees from completely resorting to their "old" culture as they would have done with previous tasks. They are thus able to compromise on a new shared way of doing things.
- Detailed implementation plan with milestones.

Conflict Management in Different Phases of Mergers & Acquisitions

Phase	Phase 1 Preparation *Planning*	Phase 2 Design *Negotiation & Transition*	Phase 3 Implementation *Integration*
Issues / Conflict	• Complexity of process is underestimated • Business environment and organization and locations • Multi vision • Self-interest of leaders • Nomination of mgmt. team • Misunderstandings • Miscommunication • Management culture/style • Personality differences • Different interests of stakeholders	• Process landscape incl. tools/systems • Organizational process • Staff **qualifications** • Nomination of positions, and economic changes • Limited resources • Core values • Decide on how to communicate • Decision making • Self-interest • Differences in organizational culture • Unclear communication • Fear and uncertainty • Respect ("us" vs. "them") • Pressure (deadlines)	• Differences in organizational culture • Communication is unclear, effective or **affirming** • Ongoing rites and rituals • Style of staff • Management style • Respect ("us" vs. "them") • Pressure (deadlines) • Self-interest
Measures	• Assign key roles • Governance structure regarding how staff and systems will integrate • Communication planning and guidelines • Analysis of cultures	• Project plan with deadlines • Create a new task on which employees from both the acquiring and acquired company work together • Communication plan • Address **conflicts** • Set expectations, maintain credibility and reinforce trust • Prevent misinformation and drama	• Implementation plan • Pro-active and transparent communication • Set expectations, maintain credibility and reinforce trust • Prevent misinformation and drama • Seek to understand by listening, asking questions, giving others a chance to tell their story

Fig. 3.2 Conflict management during M&A transaction and integration phases. Source: Bergamin/Braun, and André Sutter from SeestattExperts

How does Riet Cadonau resolve conflict? He suggests providing time and space at meetings for the so-called "elephants in the room". It is a manner of addressing conflict proactively, with the possible effect that subgroups spontaneously develop and propose solutions for further common evaluation in order to reestablish management alignment. In the singular event where no solutions can be found, Cadonau takes the decision and ensures that he substantiates it with precision.

The concept referred to as RAPID is a valuable tool in conflict avoidance or conflict solution. It defines decision processes, as many conflicts result from a lack of clarity in processes or responsibilities. The concept recommends five roles as part of the decision-making process: I for input, R for recommend, A for agree, P for perform, and D for decision. Based on the matrix organization, dormakaba introduced them instead of directives, but they can be employed in projects as well. The concept contributes towards facilitating consensus decisions. On the condition that the management lives by it and makes it daily management routine. CEO Cadonau credits the fact that he is hardly ever involved in conflict discussions to this concept. Conflicts are already resolved on a lower level. Situations where decisions are recurrently delegated upwards to him would suggest that the management staff involved should undergo further training or even be called into question (Fig. 3.3).

This interview and case study is published with the kind permission of Riet Cadonau, CEO, dormakaba Group.

3.8 The dormakaba Merger Takeaways

- Comprehensive and prudent preparation prior to closing. The contract should clarify leadership issues in particular (no double functions, no staffing parity).
- Clearly defined, fair and rapid evaluation process of the top management.

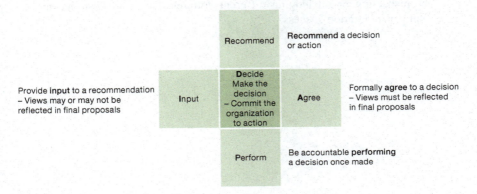

Fig. 3.3 RAPID® (is a registered trademark of Bain & Company, Inc.)—a methodology for decision making. Source: Bain & Company

- Ambitious road map in order to develop the new operating model with the previously established key players in open and unbiased meetings.
- High commitment to communication as the success factor: CEO and top management travel on site, modern communication/social media tools such as Yammer, for instance, can be valuable assets.

What are the do's and don'ts when it comes to conducting integration projects of a global scale with the collaboration of unfamiliar cultures and mentalities?

> **Bottom Line**
>
>
>
> - Involve and commit key persons as it is crucial for a rapid and effective transformation process. Guiding coalitions on the top level are mission-critical.
> - Consciously acquaint yourself with the partner culture and respect it. Do not think in terms of winner-loser dimensions.
> - Change follows the principle of "the best of both worlds"; the decision-making process should thereby be made transparent.
> - The local management should drive the local business and local integration, and at the same time support and monitor group functions.
>
>
>
> - A lack of transparency and communication in connection with other cultures may rapidly lead to misunderstandings.
> - If you do not listen to your discussion partner, many good problem-solving approaches and synergy yields are often lost.
> - Disrespecting or misjudging different cultures, laws and customs may hamper integration success.

Global Merger *LafargeHolcim*: Interview and Case Study

4.1 The Essentials of the Merger in Brief and Selected Press Commentaries

LafargeHolcim Ltd. with its brands Holcim and Lafarge is the world's largest producer of building materials and has its headquarters in Rapperswil-Jona, Switzerland. On April 7, 2014, Holcim and Lafarge announce their plans for a "merger of equals" by means of an exchange of shares. LafargeHolcim has almost 115,000 staff at the time of the merger, achieves an annual turnover of over CHF 33 billion and is present in 90 countries worldwide. Bruno Lafont is appointed new operative responsible of LafargeHolcim, and as CEO he is a prospective member of the new board of directors. Wolfgang Reitzle is a member of the Holcim board of directors of a year and—with effect of the general assembly on April 29, 2014—designated successor as Chairman of the Holcim board of directors after Rolf Soiron. Soiron resigns from office and Reitzle is subsequently appointed Chairman of the Board of the merged company. The merger of the two companies is closed on July 14, 2015, by rebranding Holcim Ltd. *LafargeHolcim Ltd.* and the additional listing of its stocks with Euronext Paris. The main goal during the period between the general assembly in spring 2014 and the final merger decision in summer 2015 is to obtain the approval of the competition authorities and to accomplish the sale of parts of the companies, as a condition for antitrust approval.

The strategic and industrial reasoning behind this merger is perfectly convincing. Its main focus is to take a step towards more consolidation, to employ synergies and to expand a company's global presence in a market that is characterized by immense excess capacities worldwide. A "merger of equals" as such, however, is a more tempestuous operation than perhaps thought; the risks involved in a "merger of equals" have also been a subject of discussion in the media. Should the merger be branded a failure, Holcim and Lafarge will unceremoniously join the ranks of mega fusions with European companies aboard that have failed before they were even implemented. In 2016, for instance, following considerable disagreement concerning the management of the new company, Publicis Groupe SA and

Omnicom Group Inc. called off their USD 35 billion merger on an equal footing; the merger would have created the world's largest advertising giant. Just 4 years earlier, in 2012, BAE Systems Plc and the now called Airbus Group NV were forced to abandon their merger plans upon intervention of the German Chancellor Angela Merkel.[1]

Forming a new company identity and company culture is one of the main challenges when it comes to mergers and acquisitions. Bilanz, a bi-weekly business magazine published in Zürich, Switzerland, affirms one of the issues of the LafargeHolcim merger: "The government in Paris wants a company that is as French as possible, the Swiss want it to be distinctly Swiss. Meanwhile, the new group has long been globally oriented".[2]

The most central decisions of former Holcim Chairman of the Board, Soiron, soon were to be reconsidered; and Wolfgang Reitzle and Bruno Lafont did not hold their offices for long. The personal chemistry and suitability profile were not in line with the expectations held. The period in question is now generally referred to as a lost year.[3] The merger now seems to build up momentum, notably in a second run-up.

The most significant events of the merger in chronological order:

> **April 7, 2014: Announcement of the merger**
> Wolfgang Reitzle takes over as Chairman of the Board; Bruno Lafont is appointed Chief Executive Officer (CEO). Closing of the transaction requires the approval of the competition authorities. Antitrust issues subsequently call for the divestment of various locations in several countries.
>
> **February/March 2015: New conditions for the completion of the merger**
> Early 2015 raises two important topics that threaten a successful completion of the transaction: Holcim wishes to appoint a CEO from its own ranks, and at the same time requires to renegotiate the exchange rate of shares in this share deal transaction. Jean-Jacques Gauthier, former Chief Financial Officer (CFO) of Lafarge, takes over internally as Chief Integration Officer.
>
> **April 2015: Appointment of the new leadership team**
> A new leadership team is selected; Eric Olsen is appointed CEO, Thomas Aebischer takes over as CFO. Former Lafarge CEO Bruno Lafont—originally intended for the position of CEO—now joins Wolfgang Reitzle as Co-chairman of the Board. Bernard Fontana, the acting Holcim CEO leaves the company.

(continued)

---

[1]Bilanz (2015, March 18), also see NZZ (2016, August 6).
[2]Bilanz (2015, July 29).
[3]Bilanz (2016, 25–26, p. 22ff).

July 14, 2015: Closing the merger
The approval of the competition authorities and clarification of the exchange rate means that the merger can go full steam ahead.

October 12, 2015: New CFO
Shortly after the announcement of the merger, an external candidate is appointed CFO.

March 2016: The merger is sluggish
The integration process is slow. No more than a third of all divestment plans have been implemented so far. The remaining divestments are to be realized by the end of 2016. The capital market is dissatisfied with the merger activities to date.

May 2016: The new group management is announced
The group management is to undergo further changes. Ian Thackwray, head of Asia, and Alain Bourguignon, head of North America are discharged due to performance issues. At the same time, Wolfgang Reitzle steps down as member of the board of directors and Beat Hess takes over.

July 2017: New CEO
CEO Eric Olsen resigns, and Jan Jenisch is appointed new CEO.

4.2 Interview with Christof Hässig, Head of Strategy and M&A, LafargeHolcim

From today's point of view and roughly 2 years after the LafargeHolcim merger, what experiences and conclusions can be drawn from the integration phase? What went according to plan? Were there any surprises or major challenges?

Christof Hässig: The industrial reasoning behind the merger of Holcim and Lafarge makes perfect sense. The further integration efforts progress, the more evident are the benefits of this merger. The cement market's excess capacities indeed present a major challenge, as 4 billion tons of capacity contrast with a 3-billion-ton demand. China, with 700 million tons, and Europe and South America with 300 million tons, share these 1-billion-ton excess capacities. India, on the other hand, lacks the necessary production capacities. The preparatory steps that the competition authorities required to proceed with the merger were implemented without further ado. All subsequent integration efforts, however, do take time. Several attempts were needed to establish the management of the joint enterprise. Economic development in crucial markets, such as Brazil, Nigeria, some EU countries, Indonesia, Egypt and the Gulf states, is difficult, which also challenges the company in terms of financial communication.[4] *What is more, the characteristics of a "merger of equals" set particular requirements when it comes to consensus-building. The equal representation of both companies in the new committees undoubtedly has had a detrimental effect on the integration process.*

Early integration planning is decisive in integration management. How did LafargeHolcim tackle the integration phase?

Christof Hässig: LafargeHolcim initiated integration planning early on with the assistance of McKinsey. Formal planning only, however, revealed to fall short; it is just as important to set the goals that need to be attained. For that reason, any top management ought to address and discuss their future strategy straightaway. If this step is omitted, ambiguities will breed speculation and as a result hamper the integration process. In the case of LafargeHolcim, the management initially focused on tackling competition issues and the sale of business areas. Strategy issues were neglected. Looking back, this nonchalance in terms of strategy discussion unfortunately set the company back a good 6 months. This pending matter has now been settled and there is a strategy road map, transparency has been created and the management agrees on what the priorities are.

According to Hässig, alignment in the top management is what makes or breaks integration success. This, however, requires a positive general attitude of those involved and a positive cultural environment. People ultimately decide on the outcome of a merger. Various factors, such as its French business culture, but also the particular setting of a "merger of equals" and subsequent discussions, analyses and reviewing of decisions that had already been taken led to delays in the integration process of LafargeHolcim. These issues also prompted unexpected cases of replacement; the integration officer and former Lafarge CEO, for instance, soon had to relinquish his position.

The role of integration officer institutionalizes the accountabilities of an integration process. LafargeHolcim's awareness of this fact made the company appoint the position at an early stage during the process. What skills and qualities does a chief integration officer have to bring to the table? Hässig maintains that the profile of an integration officer includes a vital managerial function that goes beyond its mere analyzing and planning purpose. It is thus this managerial function that ultimately decides on the integration officer's success. Hässig claims that albeit an integration officer's planning responsibilities are crucial, integration officers actually are key motivators of the integration process. Analytical skills and structural knowhow can simply be purchased in the form of an external consultant. An integration officer, on the other hand, must be equipped with the emotional skills that can govern this momentous process of change actively. Motivation, the right atmosphere and enthusiasm are vital elements that embrace employees and spark their passionate commitment. Integration officers need to be prepared to expose themselves and set guiding integration principles. This quality in particular soon called for the restaffing of this key role at LafargeHolcim.

---

[4]Bilanz (2016, March 17).

4.2 Interview with Christof Hässig, Head of Strategy and M&A, LafargeHolcim

How does project management approach different cultural backgrounds and mentalities?

Christof Hässig: The "merger of equals" is a challenge, as three different cultural backgrounds and mentalities clash around the main shareholders: the consensus and long-term-oriented Swiss with their decentralized reasoning, the hierarchical French and their centralized way of thinking, and the profit-oriented Egyptians with a short-term view.[5] Hässig confirms that albeit cultural differences exist, there is no such thing as one suitable culture only. Every cultural background and mentality has its issues. He therefore advocates openness and acceptance with regard to dissenting cultural views. All participants must be prepared to focus on the strengths and shared characteristics of their different backgrounds; sadly, in many instances when two parties approach each other, their differences and weaknesses seem to take priority.

Hässig points out the importance of branding in the integration process when it comes to cultural background and mentality. A strong brand helps employees to identify with the new company. In the case of the Ciba and Geigy merger, employees would continue to identify with their original company for years. It was only the change to Novartis that helped to influence their identity. LafargeHolcim as a company name, too, retains the origins of both companies. Speculation in the media suggests that 2017 will bring a name change.[6]

LafargeHolcim has set ambitious targets with synergy yields of CHF 1.4 billion. What course of action will meet this tall order?

Christof Hässig: First of all, synergy targets must be communicated openly and transparently right from the beginning. LafargeHolcim has publicly declared that the merger is expected to yield CHF 1.4 billion from synergy effects. Under the heading of "commercial transformation" the company plans to distinguish itself from its competitors by means of innovative products.[7] Announcing the synergy targets means commitment, but actions speak louder than words.

According to Hässig, the synergy management is proceeding as planned. The synergy process was off to a sluggish start, but measures are now yielding the desired results. The synergy potentials referred to concern areas such as products, procurement as well as logistics/network optimization. Various innovation processes have also been set in motion since the merger, with a focus on the future range of products. It has been a mutual learning process that has revealed that in the future the company should additionally focus on providing entire service packages apart from products such as concrete, gravel and cement. At the same

---

[5]Bilanz (2016, 25–26, p. 24).
[6]Bilanz (2016, 25–26, p. 27). Neue Zürcher Zeitung, "Ohne Namen geht es kaum" (English: "No name, no gain"), (2016, August 5).
[7]Handelszeitung (2015, July 15).

time, LafargeHolcim is considering to venture into the construction chemistry market with new products such as insulation foam.

LafargeHolcim ascribes great importance to the idea of simplicity; the management thus is keen to simplify the integration process for each country involved. Emphasis therefore clearly is on the divestment of units in order to meet antitrust regulations, and beyond that, the company will refrain from considerable changes within the organizations in these different countries. To further adhere to the idea of simplicity, in mission critical regions, either the Lafarge or Holcim unit was divested respectively. Complicated reorganizations were consciously avoided. The extent of the changes on a corporate level, on the other hand, presents a different picture altogether. Here, the aim clearly is to standardize the organization, and prevent duplication. In addition to that, there are two headquarter structures existing alongside each other, in Paris and Zurich. According to media reports, however, this particular issue is likely to be addressed in the near future.[8]

Speed is of the essence when it comes to crucial decisions, such as the appointment of key positions or the definition of the new organization. How did LafargeHolcim proceed in this matter?

The swift appointment of key positions admittedly is important, yet it also depends on a company's individual situation. In the case of the different organizations in the various countries involved within the framework of LafargeHolcim, and particularly the units that continue to exist, there was no immediate need for decisions. However, the contrary was the case for the corporate center functions. Numerous candidates were lined up for a range of functions at LafargeHolcim, such as M&A, treasury and so on. The selection process dragged on for much too long, which meant that candidates were left in the dark for a prolonged period of time with respect to their professional future. This atmosphere of uncertainty is undoubtedly responsible for many of the upper management leaving during this time. In the top management, however, decisions were made rapidly, albeit—as has been shown—a number of functions were less straightforward to staff than others.

This interview and case study is published with the kind permission of Christof Hässig, Head of Strategy and M&A, LafargeHolcim.

4.3 Antitrust Issues and the Merger Process

Under competition authority regulation, and as a prerequisite for the conclusion of the merger, LafargeHolcim was obliged to divest previously selected subsidiaries that were expected to reach a market-dominating position.

During the phase between the signing and approval by the competition authorities, both partners are to adhere to stringent guidelines. It is therefore of

---

[8]Bilanz (2016, 25–26, p. 27).

utmost importance that no sensitive data be exchanged that might influence the competition in any way. Particularly information that might disclose details about the commercial situation and the margins of individual transactions to the partners must not be exchanged. The project teams involved must consciously be kept small. Any recruiting process for the new structure can only begin, once the competition authorities have given their approval.

So-called clean teams are employed to conduct the necessary investigations in such difficult conditions. Clean teams consist of external consultants that—upon request by the negotiating parties—obtain insight into sensitive data, which then allows them to judge the situation from an antitrust point of view. Any knowledge that a clean team gains or the conclusions drawn from it is not to be shared with the parties involved. In the case of LafargeHolcim, these clean teams consisted of around one hundred people who exchanged sensitive information that allowed them to take the relevant antitrust steps and measures.

4.4 The LafargeHolcim Merger Takeaways

The LafargeHolcim merger aptly demonstrates the complexity of a "merger of equals". The parties' readiness for equal leadership and their wish for an equal representation of their companies in their committees sets particular challenges to the leadership team. In our view, the following aspects are decisive for success:

- Due to the complexity of a "merger of equals", **rapid appointment of key roles** is decisive. Co-management solutions at the top level are to be avoided as they thwart clear leadership and considerably complicate any decision-making processes.
- The "merger of equals" typically entails a high degree of leadership complexity. For this reason, companies are well advised to **discuss a new corporate strategy** early on in the process and set their goals and the new operating model straight away. In a next step, **charisma and conviction** are required to inspire and align staff with the new strategy as a convincing way forward. The integration officer has to assume a leadership role and motivate the management.
- **Branding and strong brands** will facilitate employee identification with the new company. LafargeHolcim could therefore only benefit from establishing a new brand that no longer reflects the company's origins.[9]

---

[9] Also see: Ulrike Grein, "Marke hilft bei Integration", in: Handelszeitung, (2017, January 19, p. 41).

Bottom Line

- Rapid appointment of key roles.
- Strategy must be mapped out from the beginning.
- The integration officer has to be an excellent leader.

- Avoid co-management situations, as they complicate decision making processes and delay change.
- Avoid brand names that reflect both companies' history (LafargeHolcim). They remind employees of their former "homes" and may make them reluctant to create and embrace a new company culture.

Closing Remarks

This book addresses the topic of integration management. We adamantly believe that thriving growth companies are successful because of their relentless and enduring integration management. Beyond the actual integration project, the pulse of a process is beating incessantly aiming to continuously enforce improvement measures in the entire corporation. Looking back on almost 40 years of experience in transaction management altogether, we are convinced that these are the parameters for successful integration.

Uncounted debates and interviews in connection with this book project have over and beyond confirmed that successful companies regard themselves as organizations that strive to acquire knowledge. They are open to change and willing to move onwards and upwards. That said, people's willingness to learn largely depends on the management in place. The results of our research in the field of integration management have also made us revisit our initial view of things: We now sternly believe that (a) integration management should primarily concentrate on the actual integration project, and that (b) rapid decisions with respect to crucial topics are imperative, e.g. the appointment of key persons or the future structure of the organization. The person in charge of the operative side of the integration project is tightly involved into the M&A target process, then ensures successful integration management, and ultimately also warrants for the project phase to swiftly return to courant normal or daily business as soon as possible. Those responsible for the operative side of integration use the integration project to create momentum in the entire corporation and to foster young talents. Indecision, procrastination, non-transparency and a lack of communication are to be avoided at all cost.

M&A activity is currently intense, and integration management success stories as much as failures make the headlines on a regular basis. Everyone's eyes are on transnational acquisitions to occupy leading positions in increasingly open and accessible international markets. As is often the case, unsuccessful or problematic mergers and acquisitions are particularly susceptible to media attention. It is from these cases that we draw the following conclusions to be put into integration practice:

The design of the integration phase must be established as early as during due diligence. Before the contract is signed, the most important challenges of all ensuing integration efforts have to be pinpointed and it has to be clear how they are going to be overcome.

- Company strategy and organizational structures (change management) have to be adapted with a sense of proportion; it is all about the right mix of sense of proportion and assertiveness.
- The resources that are allocated to integration must be planned well ahead and be available. Their costs have to flow into the assessment of an M&A transaction.
- Persistent integration management monitoring ensures strict implementation of original targets. A disciplined project management is the be-all and end-all of an integration project.

Successful integration management can only take place in an environment of openness for other opinions, continuous eagerness to learn, and a solid project management. The same holds true for the project of this book. As authors, we bundled our experiences, had heated debates, searched for other views, and all this in one determined strike. We do hope that our team work as authors has been rewarding for you as a reader of this book.

Glossary

Change management Denotes all the tasks, measures and activities that significantly and comprehensively re-shape an organization across segments and content-wise to implement new strategies, structures, systems, processes or patterns of behavior.

Closing Signing of contract in an M&A transaction. At the closing, title to the property of the acquired company passes from seller to buyer.

Coaching In management teaching, coaching aims to improve management skills or promotes leadership development respectively.

Corporate finance Corporate finance is a special field of business finance that is concerned with all of the financial activities related to running a corporation. It covers areas such as due diligence, corporate funding, and especially M&A transactions.

Cross-selling Selling of complementary products and/or services.

Conditio sine qua non Indispensable condition.

Due diligence Due diligence is an assessment of a potential investment reviewing all financial records before entering into an agreement or a transaction with another party. Buyer and seller agree on the duration and extent of this audit before the closing.

Earn-out Share of the purchase price. It is profit-related and paid out after the closing.

Economies of scale Cost advantage that arises with an increase in output of a product, i.e. the greater the quantity of a product, the lower the fixed cost per unit.

Going private Withdrawal of a publicly traded company from the stock exchange.

Integration office When it comes to integration, large companies and corporations work with a project organization that as a rule has four cornerstones: the steering committee, the integration or project management office, the project implementation team, and the core process team. In small and mid-caps, project organization usually limits itself to those responsible for the operative side of the project, as well as supporting functions such as the integration manager and further project staff.

M&A Mergers and acquisitions is a general term that refers to transactions such as the purchase of one company by another, the combination of two companies to form a new company, or a corporate spin-off.

Monitoring Systematic recording and supervision of a course of action or process such as an integration process for example.

Pre-merger value Company value before the transaction.

Post-merger audit Integration controlling and rating of overall merger or acquisition success.

Scorecard Tool that measures, documents and steers company activities.

Small and mid-caps Small and medium-sized enterprises with a stock exchange or corporate value of CHF 100 million to CHF 2 billion, as opposed to large and mostly publicly traded companies.

Squeeze-out Denotes the compulsory sale of the shares of minority shareholders of a joint-stock company by a majority shareholder.

Soft skills Social skills such as ability to communicate and deal with conflict, empathy, loyalty and intercultural skills.

Suspension period Denotes the period between signing and closing of a transaction during which e.g. merger control approvals must be obtained.

Synergies "The whole is more than the sum of its parts" (Aristotle). Mergers produce synergies if the merged company activities complement each other or if they can be made more efficient. However, merger synergies may also be counterproductive, for instance, when the company cultures of two companies become antagonists.

Target Operating Model The target operating model describes the way the merged organization does business in the future.

Turnaround Successfully lead a company out of a crisis.

CPSIA information can be obtained
at www.ICGtesting.com
Printed in the USA
LVOW06*1059100817
544502LV00002B/7/P